ARTISTIC CALIFORNIA

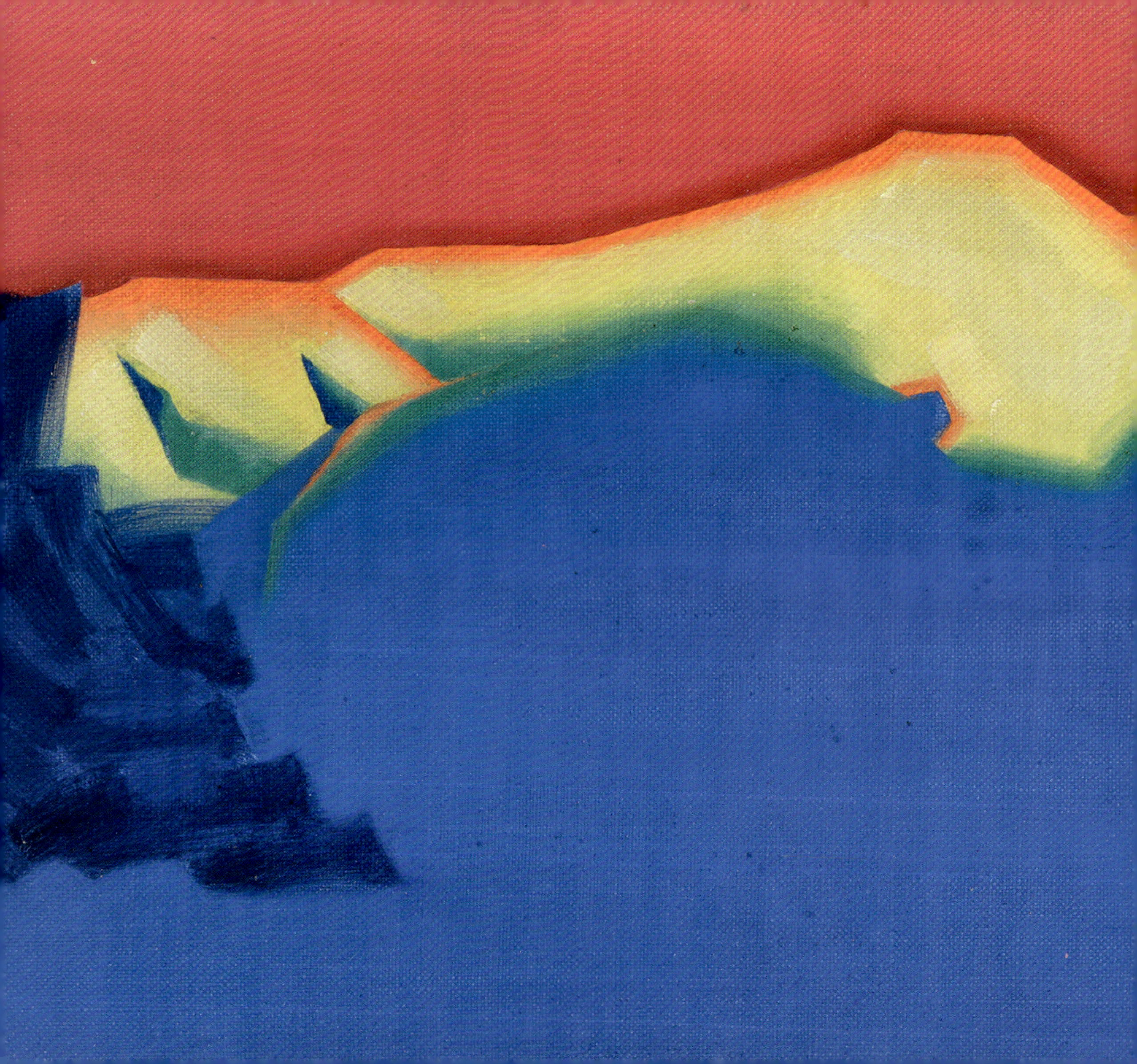

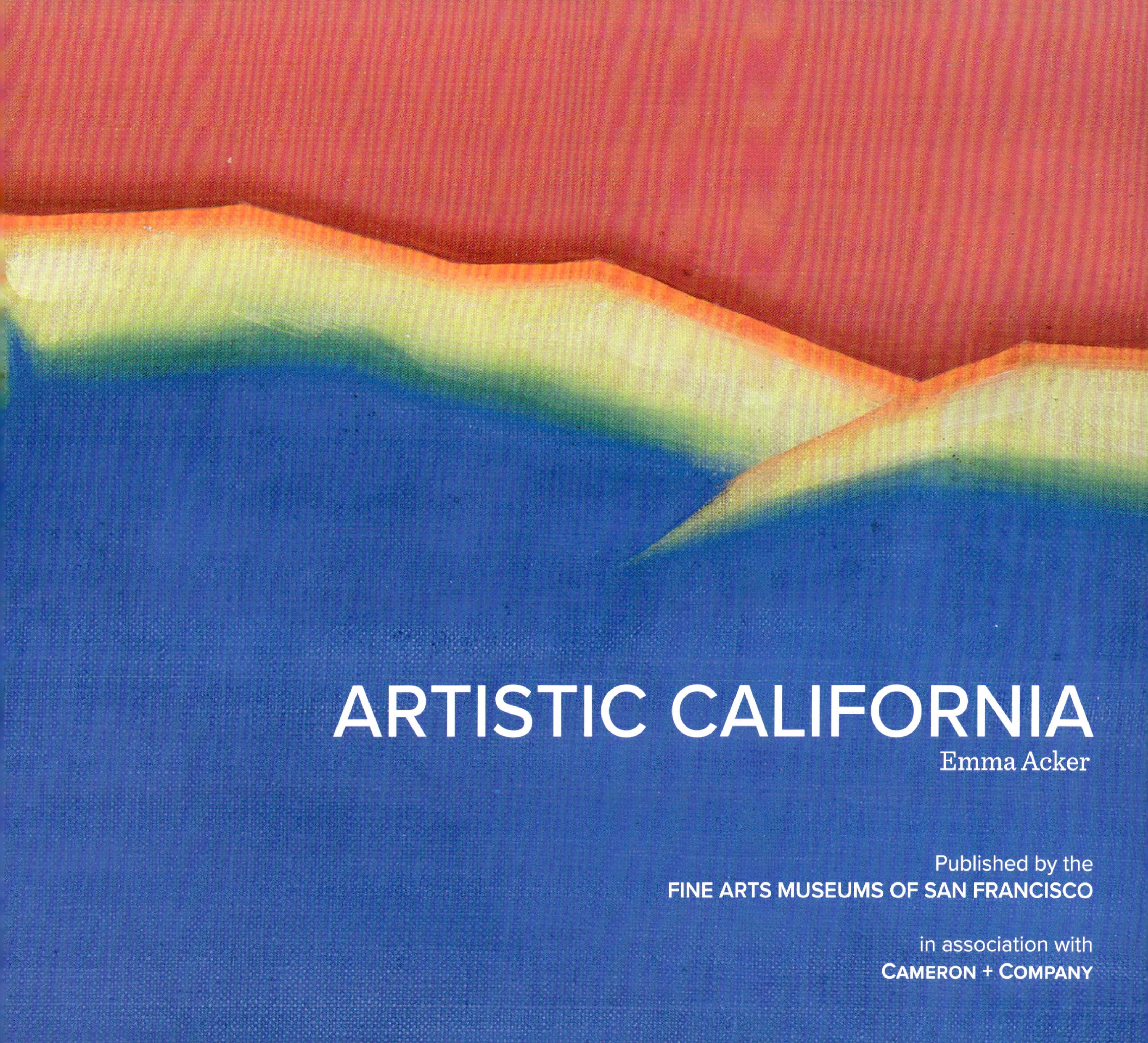

ARTISTIC CALIFORNIA

Emma Acker

Published by the
FINE ARTS MUSEUMS OF SAN FRANCISCO

in association with
CAMERON + COMPANY

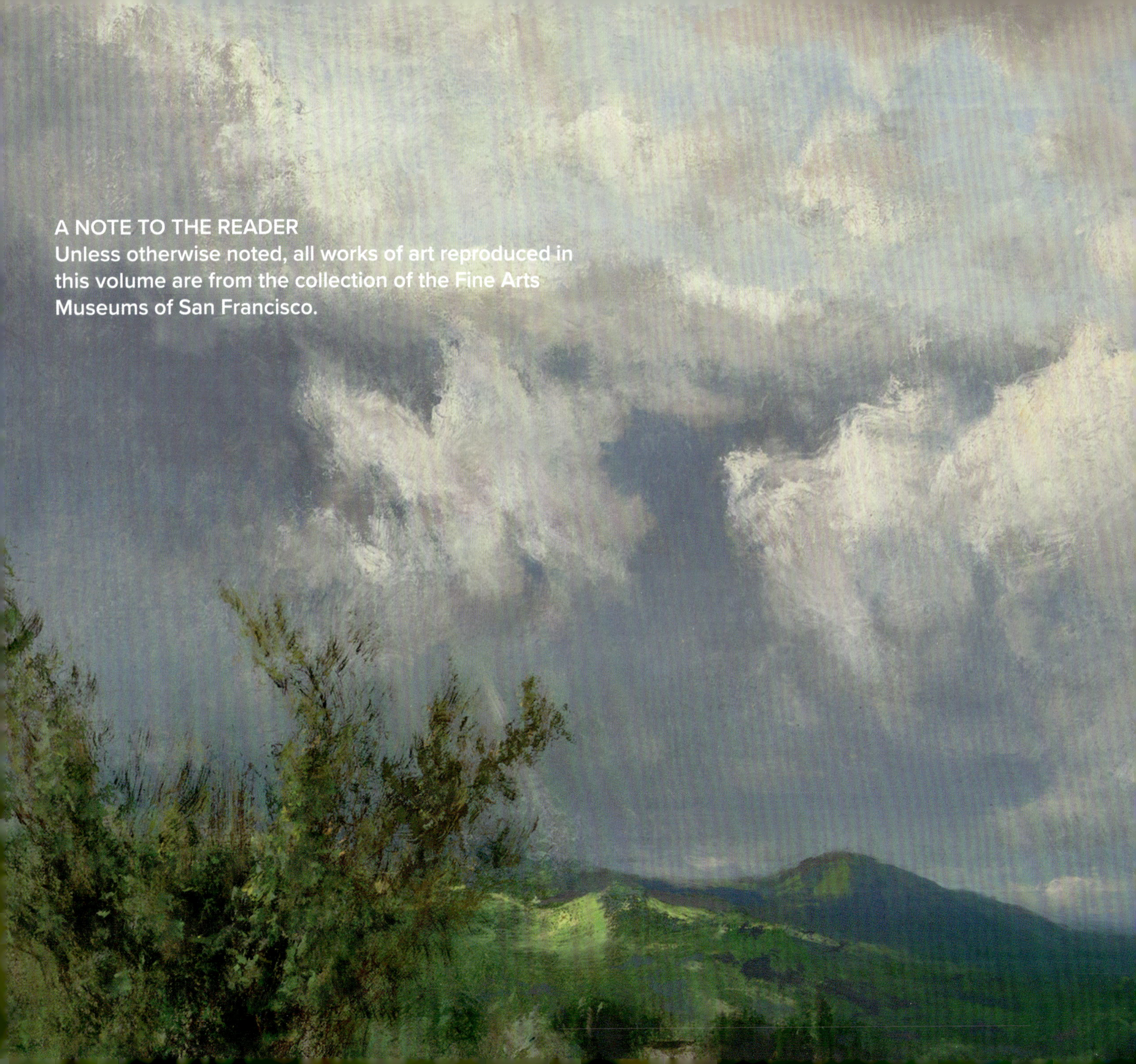

A NOTE TO THE READER

Unless otherwise noted, all works of art reproduced in this volume are from the collection of the Fine Arts Museums of San Francisco.

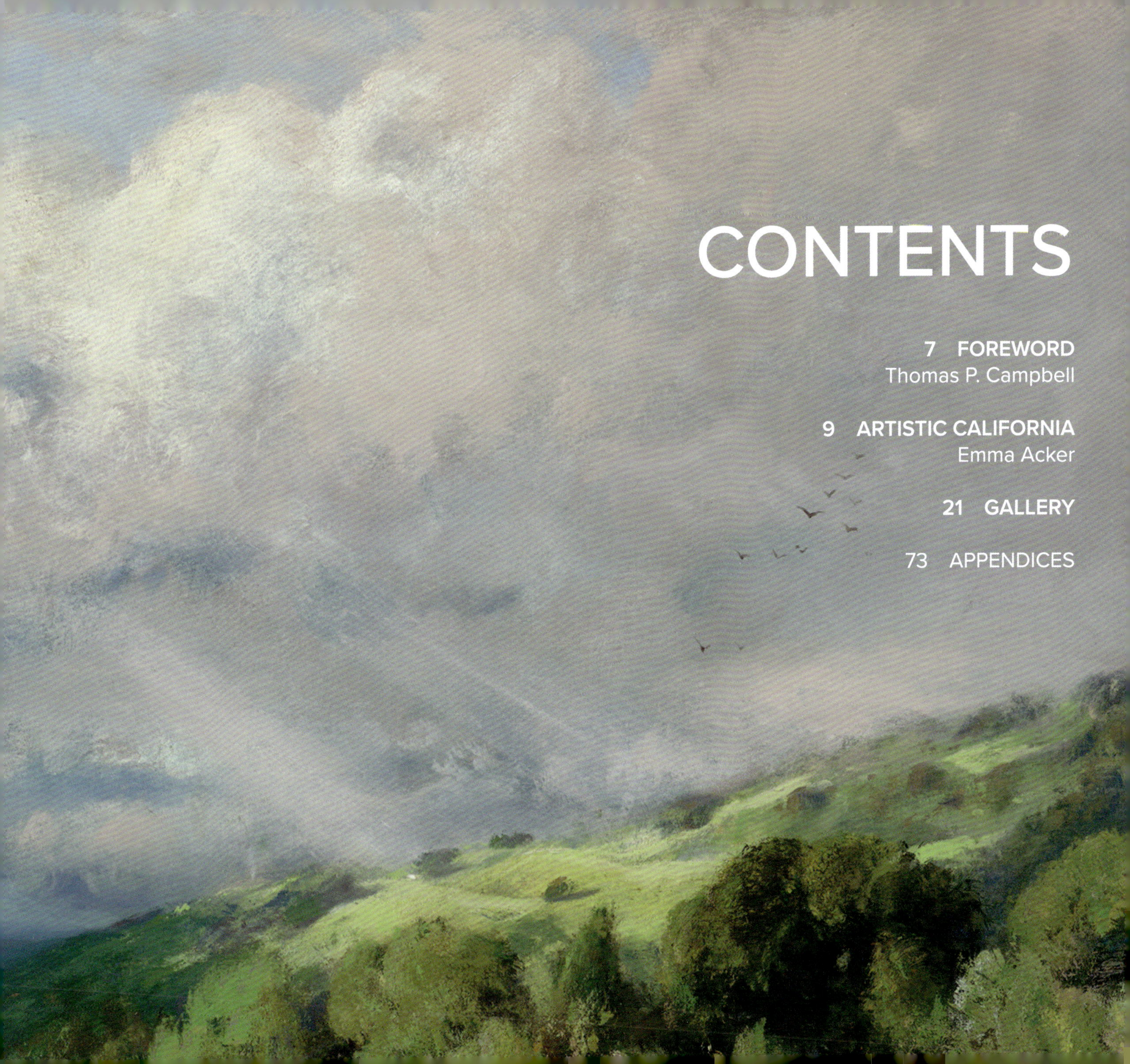

CONTENTS

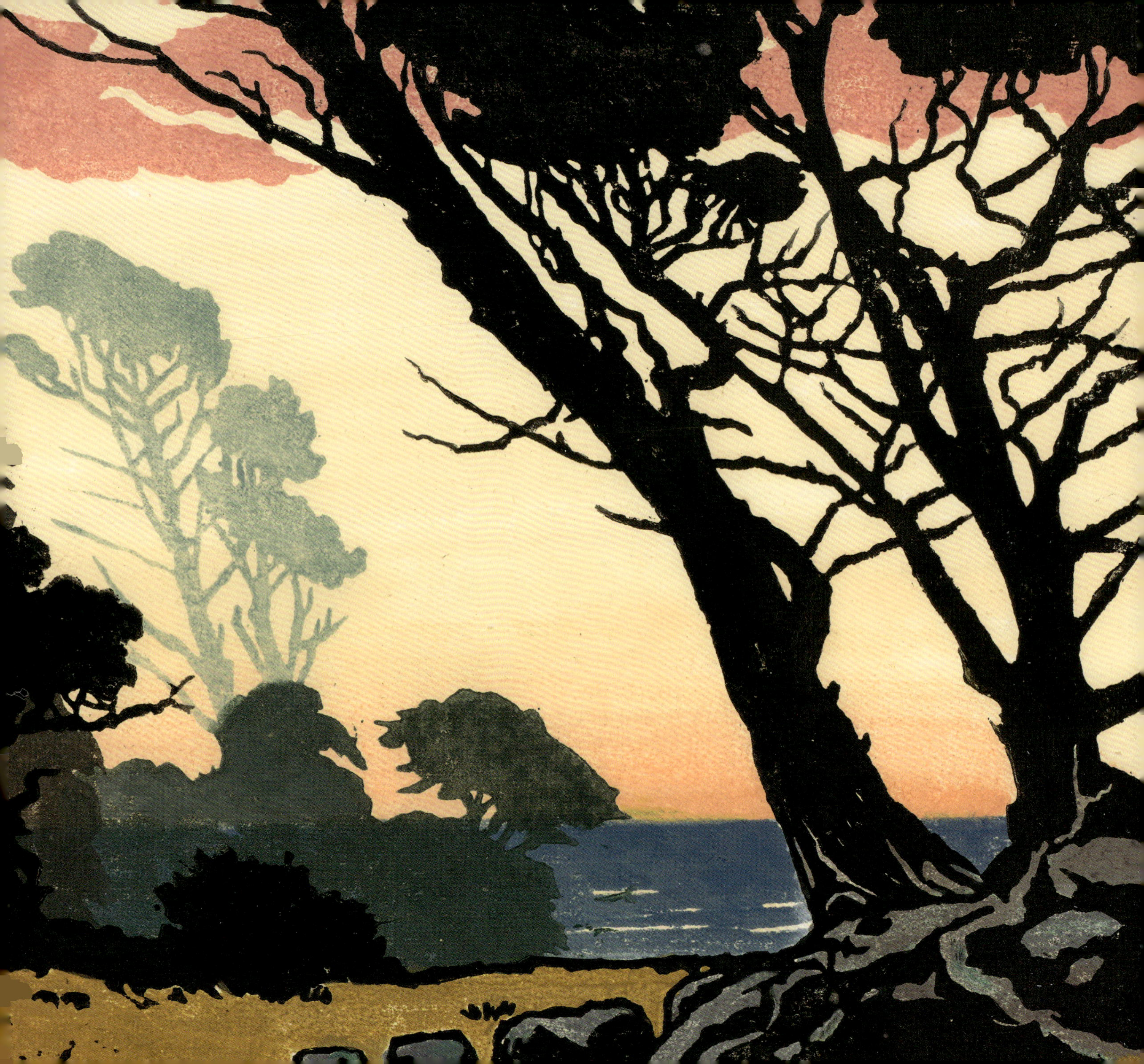

FOREWORD

Thomas P. Campbell, Director and CEO
Fine Arts Museums of San Francisco

CALIFORNIA'S BREATHTAKING LANDSCAPES, rich cultural diversity, and historic and continued embrace of innovation have inspired generations of artists, including many whose works are on view at the Fine Arts Museums of San Francisco. Art made in California remains a consistent strength of the institution's permanent collection. This includes the sweeping, panoramic scenes of the American West by nineteenth-century artists such as Albert Bierstadt; early twentieth-century plein-air scenes by Society of Six painters; and the meditative, abstracted landscapes of Chiura Obata. Also well represented in the Museums' holdings are the post–World War II innovations of artists such as Robert Bechtle, Bernice Bing, Joan Brown, Jay DeFeo, Richard Diebenkorn, Richard Mayhew, Ed Ruscha, and Wayne Thiebaud, among many others. The Museums likewise have a dedicated track record of supporting California artists. Noteworthy in the institution's history are the Group *f*.64 exhibition at the M.H. de Young Memorial Museum in 1932, Diebenkorn's solo exhibition at the Legion of Honor museum in 1948, and an Obata retrospective in 2000, as well as the creation of a permanent installation of Ruth Asawa's magnificent looped- and tied-wire sculptures for the new de Young museum in 2005. This legacy continues today with initiatives such as the triennial juried exhibition of art produced in the Bay Area, *The de Young Open*.

Underscoring the scope and quality of the Museums' collection, the works featured in *Artistic California* collectively offer a dynamic and multifaceted portrait of the state. Many of the paintings and works on paper that are reproduced in this book celebrate the stunning natural beauty of a region that encompasses all the major climates found on Earth except an arctic or tropical zone, fostering ecosystems that nourish an incredible array of flora and fauna. The essay authored by Emma Acker, associate curator of American art, sheds light on California's artistic heritage, as well as its complex and layered histories. The utopian idealism and positive outlook that has historically existed in California persists to this day, fueling its residents' unceasing quests for technological breakthroughs; social evolution and revolution; and personal, professional, and creative growth. With headquarters for two of the most influential industries in the world — entertainment and technology — California is at the forefront of shaping social and economic trends in the United States and beyond. Yet the region is also an epicenter for many of America's gravest challenges, including surging wealth gaps and unhoused populations and the catastrophic impacts of climate change. Art produced in California reveals the vibrancy and diversity of the region's people and places, while also reflecting these complex issues and how our understanding of them has changed over time.

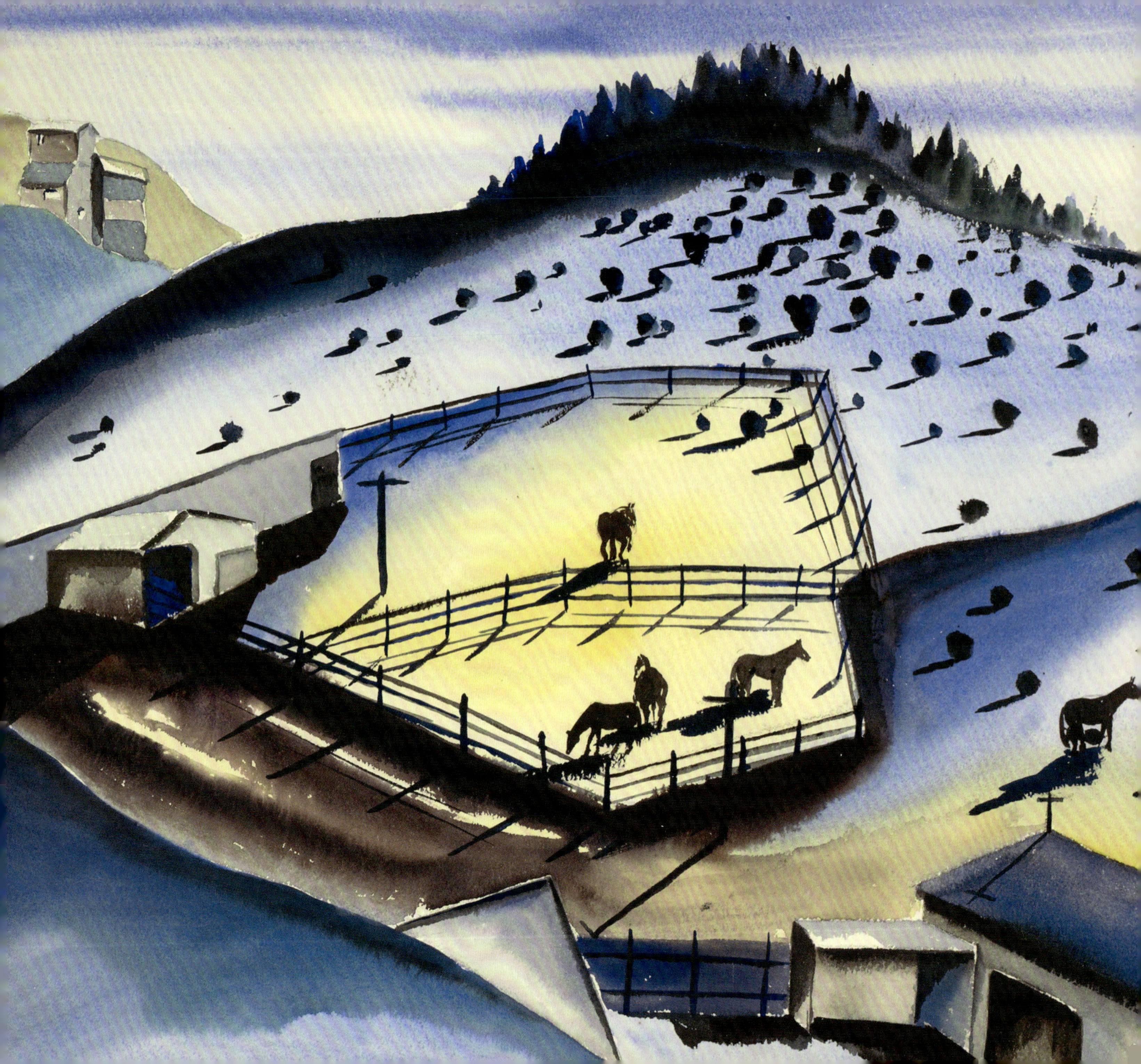

ARTISTIC CALIFORNIA

Emma Acker

NAMED FOR A MYTHICAL ISLAND featured in a sixteenth-century Spanish chivalric romance novel, California has long been associated with fantasy and wish fulfillment.[1] Perennially envisioned as a land of promise, this vast, populous crossroads for diverse topographies and cultures continues to attract dreamers and innovators of all kinds, including visual artists seeking inspiration in the region's vibrant communities and resplendent landscapes. California's dramatically varied geography, formed from the collision of two major tectonic plates and their subsequent movements over millions of years, provides an enticing repertoire of artistic subjects — including the 1,264-mile Pacific shoreline, majestic mountain ranges, primeval redwood forests, and arid desert interiors.

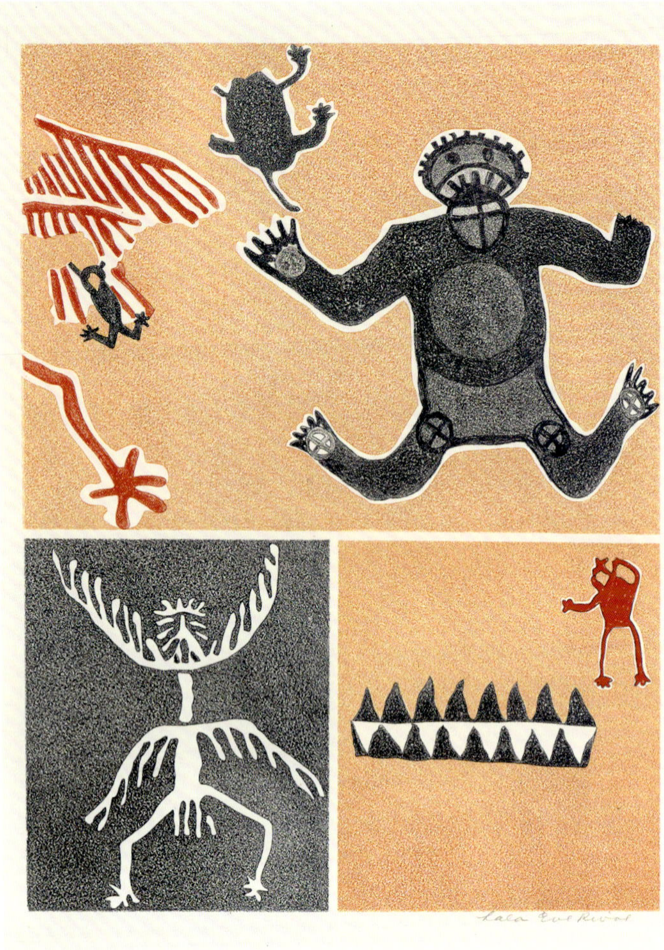

1 | Lala Eve Rivol (1913–1996), *Petroglyph: Mutau Flat, Ventura County, California*, ca. 1935–1938. Color lithograph, 14 5/8 x 11 1/8 in. (37.2 x 28.2 cm). Allocated by the Federal Art Project, L43.2.588

Throughout California's history, artists have helped shape the way the region is seen by its residents and the wider world. Once uncritically celebrated and promoted as an Edenic paradise, California is now more readily understood as a place of contradictions and coexistence. California's dichotomous image encompasses natural majesty and suburban sprawl, expanse and congestion, abundance and want, counterculture and conformism, diversity and exclusion, and glamour and grit. Variously reflecting, burnishing, constructing, or deconstructing the mythologies underpinning conceptions of the Golden State, artists working in California have communicated an ever-shifting sense of regional identity influenced by their historical moment, artistic training and aesthetic preferences, and personal experiences and perspectives.

The longevity of California's rich artistic legacy is manifest in the magnificent petroglyphs and pictographs, the earliest of which may date to about 10,000 BCE, that were created by the Native Californians who first settled the region thousands of years ago. Featuring enigmatic human, animal, and celestial forms as well as other abstracted designs, these rock carvings are thought to depict mythological, cosmological, or historical events. They may have served a religious or ceremonial function, marked territorial boundaries, or indicated the presence of natural resources. In a series of lithographs she produced during the Great Depression for the Federal Art Project, San Francisco–based artist Lala Eve Rivol documented many of these artworks, some of which were subsequently damaged by natural forces or desecration. This print by Rivol features pictographs painted by the Chumash people on Mutau Flats Rock in the Topatopa Mountains of Ventura County (fig. 1).

The coastal Chumash belonged to one of more than one hundred Indigenous cultural groups who thrived on the lands now encompassed by the state of California when European explorers

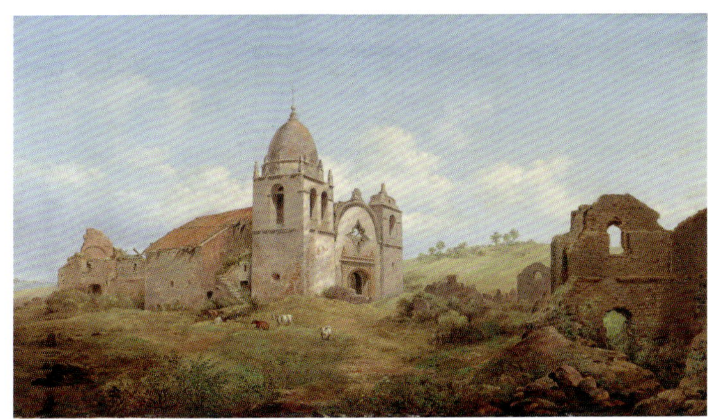

2 | Juan Buckingham Wandesforde (1817–1902), *Mission San Carlos Borromeo Del Carmelo*, 1875. Oil on canvas, 38 1/2 x 67 5/8 in. (97.8 x 171.8 cm). Gift of the Friends of the Museum in memory of Frank S. Douty, 43150

first arrived in 1542, led by Juan Rodríguez Cabrillo on behalf of Spain.[2] Over two centuries later, during the Spanish colonial era (1769–1821), a sustained European presence took root in Alta California, as the region was then known.[3] Beginning in 1769, Spanish missionaries led by the Franciscan priest Junípero Serra established twenty-one missions on or near the California coast, each a day's journey apart, stretching from San Diego to Sonoma. Aided by designs in Mexican architectural books that were supplied by the Franciscan friars, Native Californians constructed the missions out of adobe, sometimes embellishing their interiors with hand-painted frescoes. Although in reality this period was marked by extreme brutality and the systematic subjugation of Indigenous communities, later generations of Californians frequently romanticized life under Spanish, and subsequently Mexican (1821–1846), rule.[4] Nineteenth-century architectural preservationists sought to restore the missions, while many artists depicted the structures as picturesque ruins (fig. 2).

In the mid-nineteenth century, fueled by the expansionist ideology of Manifest Destiny, waves of Anglo-American pioneers trekked west to settle in California. Among them were members of the Donner Party, many of whom infamously perished after becoming snowbound in the Sierra Nevada mountains in the winter of 1846–1847. In *View of Donner Lake, California* (1871–1872), the German-born American landscape painter Albert

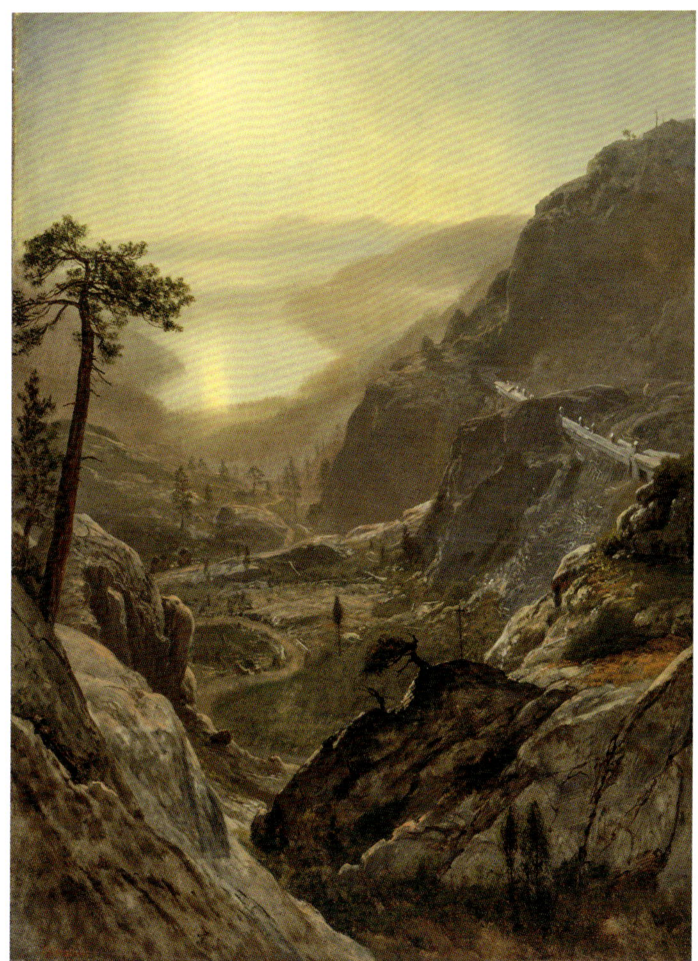

3 | Albert Bierstadt (1830–1902), *View of Donner Lake, California*, 1871–1872. Oil on paper mounted on canvas, 29 1/4 x 21 7/8 in. (74.3 x 55.6 cm). Gift of Anna Bennett and Jessie Jonas in memory of August F. Jonas, Jr., 1984.54

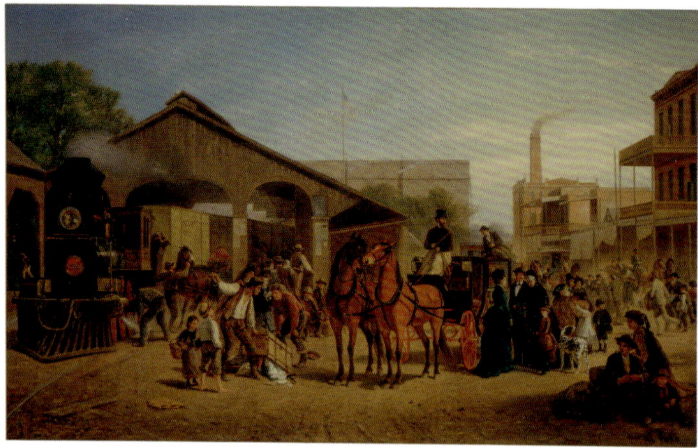

4 | William Hahn (1829–1887), *Sacramento Railroad Station*, 1874. Oil on canvas, 53 ¾ x 87 ¾ in. (136.5 x 222.9 cm). Museum purchase, M.H. de Young Endowment Fund, 54936

Bierstadt included a small cross at center right to commemorate the lives lost during this ill-fated passage (fig. 3). The sublime landscape imagery in the painting is suffused with a luminous, rosy glow, and suggests that despite the hardships of their traversal, those who survived the perilous journey would be blessed and protected in this "promised land." *View of Donner Lake, California* is a study for Bierstadt's monumental *Donner Lake from the Summit* (1873), which was commissioned by Collis Potter Huntington, who helped finance the construction of the first railroad to cross Donner Pass in Northern California. In *View of Donner Lake, California*, Bierstadt alluded to the technological conquest of this breathtaking but notoriously treacherous part of the transcontinental Overland Route by including a row of snow sheds, perched precipitously atop the tracks at right, which facilitated the railroad's passage through massive snow drifts.[5]

The steady stream of newcomers to California became a flood following the discovery of gold on January 24, 1848, at Sutter's Mill in Coloma, on the South Fork of the American River. After President James K. Polk announced the discovery to Congress in December of that year, the regional gold rush became an international phenomenon, transforming Northern California's economy, demographics, and infrastructure overnight. Thousands of miners arrived from across the United States, Europe, China, South America, and elsewhere, eager to cash in on the riches — inaugurating the first of the many boom-and-bust cycles for which California is now notorious, and increasing the region's existing cultural diversity.[6] Towns such as Stockton, Sacramento, and, most significantly, San Francisco became important supply centers during the gold rush, their populations burgeoning in lockstep with the bonanza. California's admission as the thirty-first state of the union in 1850; the discovery of the Comstock Lode of silver ore on the eastern slopes of the Sierra Nevada in 1859; and the completion of the first transcontinental railroad, whose western terminus was in Sacramento, in 1869, further contributed to the rapid settlement of the region (fig. 4).

Among the migrants flocking to these developing frontier towns were artists, attracted by new subjects, an emerging patron base, and the establishment of arts organizations — including the San Francisco Art Union in 1851, the San Francisco Art Association in 1871, the Bohemian Club of San Francisco in 1872, and the California School of Design in 1874. Some artists, like the German-born Charles Christian Nahl, intended to make their fortunes as miners but found more success painting genre scenes and portraits of prospectors and wealthy Californians. Nahl's depiction of Peter Quivey, a migrant to California who briefly joined the Donner Party before fighting in the Mexican-American War and settling in San Jose, presents the pioneer as a mediator between the frontier and civilization (fig. 5).[7] Quivey's fringed buckskin suit, bowie knife, and Colt revolver, along with the mountain lion in the foreground, all emphasize his identity as a frontiersman reminiscent of Daniel Boone and

Davy Crockett — a persona that belies his status as an urban sophisticate and patron of the arts.

Landscape painting also flourished in California in the latter half of the nineteenth century. Some artists, such as the Scottish-born Tonalist painter William Keith, settled permanently in California (pls. 2 and 4). Others made temporary sojourns to the state — including Bierstadt, who returned to the East Coast to exhibit his California landscapes to a curious public.[8] Bierstadt's panoramic views effectively served as advertisements for the state, presenting the California landscape as an American Eden destined for future settlement. Replete with cattle grazing peacefully in verdant pastures near the Sacramento River, *California Spring* (1875) presents an idealized vision of life in the Central Valley that overlooks harsh realities such as recurrent droughts, flooding, and a landscape depleted by overgrazing (pl. 1). Silhouetted against a dazzlingly luminous sky, the faintly visible dome of the Sacramento state capitol on the horizon underscores California's growing political importance to the nation.[9]

Artistic boosterism persisted in the ensuing decades, as paintings and prints of California landscapes joined commercial posters and brochures in encouraging westward migrations and tourism to the region. Many of these scenes are devoid of human presence and portray the western landscape as unspoiled and ripe for exploration. Yet popular photographs from the era, particularly those taken in Yosemite, often contain figures posed vertiginously in the natural landscape. In George Fiske's image of a couple standing at the edge of Overhanging Rock at Glacier Point, the small scale of the figures relative to the awe-inspiring vistas that surround them conveys a sense of the precariousness and sublimity of the experience (pl. 3). Thanks to the lobbying efforts of the naturalist John Muir — as well as those of the Southern Pacific Railroad, which was invested in increasing ridership — Yosemite became a national park in 1890 and was soon one of the top tourist destinations in America.

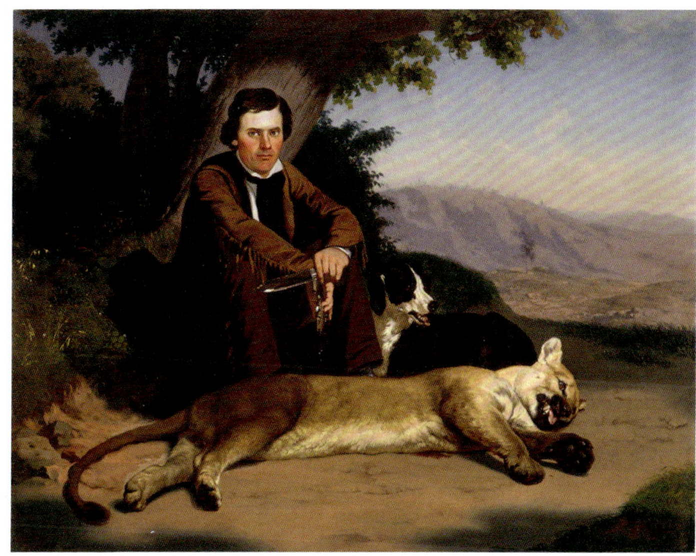

5 | Charles Christian Nahl (1818–1878), *Peter Quivey and the Mountain Lion*, 1857. Oil on canvas, 26 x 34 in. (66 x 86.4 cm). Museum purchase, James E. Harrold, Jr. Bequest Fund, and gift of Carol W. Casey, 1998.32

Following the 1906 San Francisco earthquake and fire, many artists decamped to the bohemian enclaves of Monterey and Carmel-by-the-Sea, where they produced Impressionist- and Post-Impressionist-inspired views of the California coastline and seaside villages. Like nineteenth-century western landscapes, these scenes are typically depopulated, belying a dramatic increase in coastal real estate development in California at the turn of the twentieth century. Yet the views are often more intimate than the sweeping vistas favored by earlier artists such as Bierstadt, and many were painted en plein air. Writers were also drawn to the Central Coast, including Jack London, who described the artist's colony centered in Carmel in his novel *The Valley of the Moon* (1913), and later John Steinbeck, who chronicled the misadventures and friendships of the lively denizens of Monterey in novels such as *Tortilla Flat* (1935) and *Cannery Row* (1945).

The influential artist, architect, and teacher Arthur Frank Mathews was a frequent visitor to Monterey. Along with his wife, Lucia Kleinhans Mathews, he popularized the California Decorative Style, an outgrowth of the Arts and Crafts movement. At their San Francisco gallery the Furniture Shop, they sold their handcrafted and hand-painted objects, which frequently combined classical Arcadian themes and stylized figures with views of the California landscape (fig. 6). Many printmakers working in Northern California in the early twentieth century, including Pedro J. Lemos, Frank Morley Fletcher, Frances Hammell Gearhart, and William Seltzer Rice, were also greatly influenced by the Arts and Crafts style and by traditional Japanese woodblock techniques incorporating thick outlines and flat planes of color (pls. 11, 14, 15, 21, and 22).

In the East Bay, the Society of Six — an association of Oakland-based plein-air painters who banded together in 1917 — adopted a more avant-garde aesthetic, relative to the generally conservative trends in early twentieth-century California landscape painting. Influenced partly by the modern European art movements represented at the 1915 San Francisco Panama-Pacific International Exposition, members of the group, such as Selden Connor Gile, incorporated expressionistic brushwork and a vivid, nonnatural palette into their work to capture the rugged vitality of the Northern California landscape (pl. 5). Such modernist approaches to landscape painting continued into the 1920s and 1930s. In *Mt. Tamalpais* (1927), the Japanese American artist Teikichi Hikoyama adopted a flattened perspective influenced by Japanese ukiyo-e prints, elegantly fusing landscape with figure in his streamlined composition (pl. 7).[10] The Japanese American artist Chiura Obata similarly reconciled the influences of European modernism and traditional Japanese art in works such as

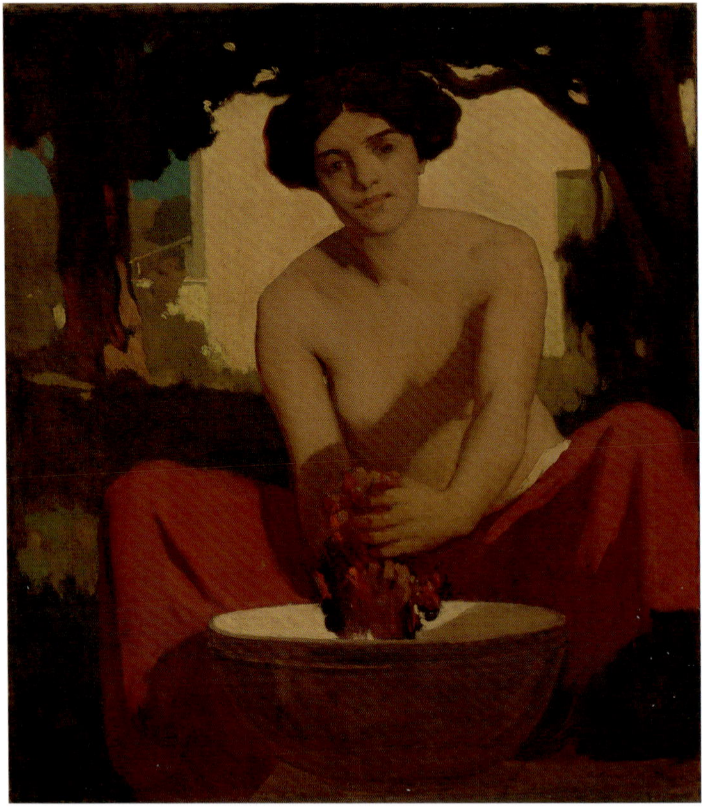

6 | Arthur Frank Mathews (1860–1945), *The Grape (The Wine Maker)*, ca. 1906. Oil on canvas, 26 x 24 in. (66 x 61 cm). Gift of Mrs. Henrietta Zeile, 37656

Lake Basin in the High Sierra (ca. 1930; pl. 8).[11] While the painting was inspired by his 1927 visit to a specific site near Tuolumne Meadows in Yosemite, Obata employed a contemplative, distilled representation of the scene to convey a universal experience of nature as an elemental and spiritually sustaining encounter.

In the early twentieth century, California artists' tendency to focus on views of pristine or idealized nature — as opposed to cultivated landscapes or built environments — paradoxically coincided with an intense period of urban and suburban expansion, in addition to the emergence of major industries such as Hollywood entertainment, oil, and agriculture. Dubbed the "Cornucopia of the World," California experienced the astronomical growth of its farming industry, beginning with wheat in the nineteenth century, then shifting by the early twentieth century to produce such as citrus. Yet landscape artists of the period rarely pictured the laborers who toiled ceaselessly, tilling fields and picking the fruits and vegetables that were then shipped across the nation in crates bearing colorful and exoticized labels advertising their origins in the Golden State (pl. 12).

With the onset of the Great Depression (1929–1939), artists turned their attention more urgently to the American social and political landscape, producing agricultural and industrial scenes that more frequently included workers or illustrated labor conflicts (fig. 7). During the 1930s, figurative compositions and social themes predominated the government-sponsored mural projects that proliferated in California, where Mexican artists David Alfaro Siqueiros, José Clemente Orozco, Alfredo Ramos Martínez, and Diego Rivera traveled to complete ambitious commissions.[12]

Many photographers working during the Great Depression similarly reflected social concerns in their work, including, perhaps most famously, Dorothea Lange, in her series of images of migrants to California from the Dust Bowl. Others embraced modernist experimentation, focusing their attention on aesthetic characteristics that are inherent to the medium of photography. The Oakland-based Group *f.*64, whose members included Ansel Adams, Imogen Cunningham (pl. 38), and Edward Weston, espoused sharp-focus "straight photography." Although not a member of Group *f.*64, Alma Lavenson was included in their inaugural exhibition at the de Young museum in 1932. While earlier in her career, Lavenson was influenced by the dreamy Pictorialist style, in later photographs she captured with crisp

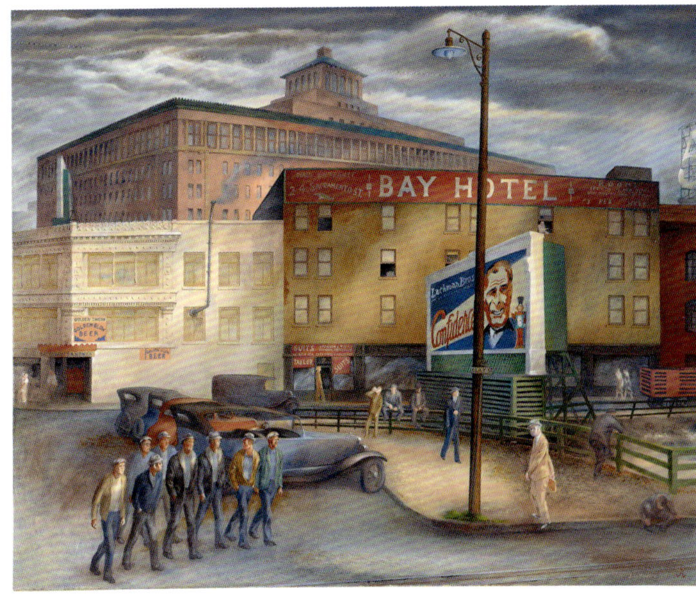

7 | John Langley Howard (1902–1999), *Embarcadero and Clay Street*, 1935. Oil on canvas, 35 ⅞ x 43 ½ in. (91.1 x 110.5 cm). Museum purchase, Dr. Leland A. Barber and Gladys K. Barber Fund, 2002.96

precision the elegant geometries of both natural and industrial forms (pl. 37).

The years leading up to and immediately following America's entry into World War II witnessed the explosive growth of California's aircraft and shipbuilding industries, and a subsequent period of economic prosperity and suburban development. A generation of American veterans attended colleges and universities with funding from the 1944 GI Bill of Rights, among them Richard Diebenkorn.[13] Born in Portland, Oregon, but raised in the Ingleside Terraces neighborhood of San Francisco, Diebenkorn was deeply rooted in the Bay Area. In the abstract works he produced in his Berkeley series (1953–1956), Diebenkorn reconciled his sensory and emotional absorption of the Northern California landscape with the influence of Abstract Expressionism (pl. 29).

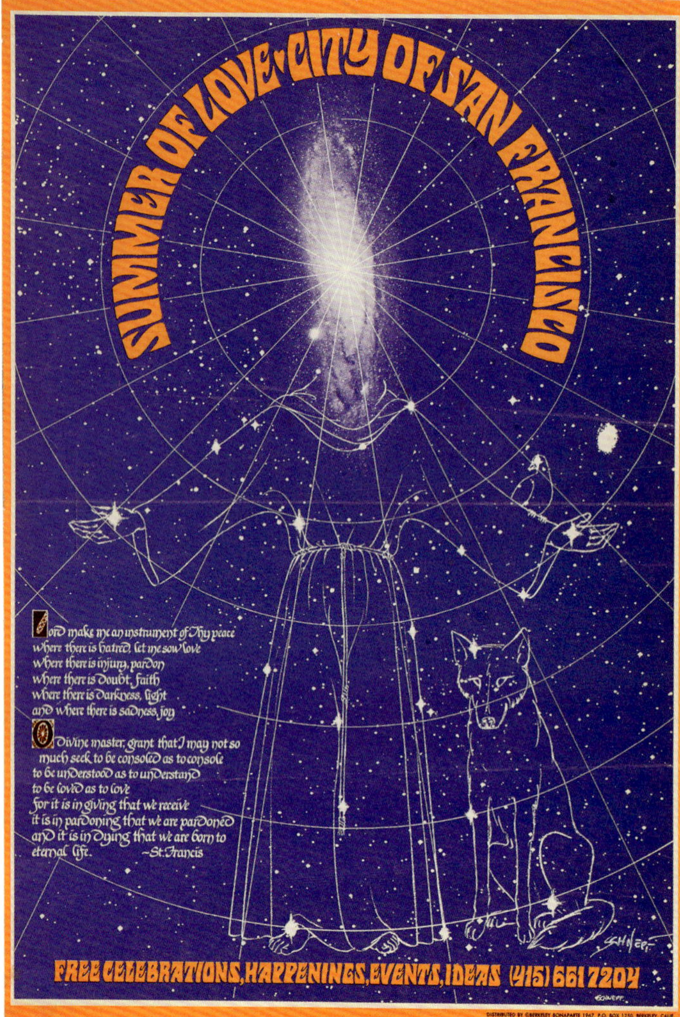

8 | Bob Schnepf (b. 1937), *Summer of Love / City of San Francisco*, 1967. Color offset lithograph poster, 20 1/2 x 14 1/16 in. (52 x 35.7 cm). Gift of the Gary Westford Collection, in honor of Bob (Raf) Schnepf, 2017.7.11

Diebenkorn was immersed in this artistic style — which emerged in Manhattan in the 1940s and predominated the New York–centered art world in the mid-twentieth century — as a student and later a teacher at the California School of Fine Arts (CSFA, later the San Francisco Art Institute).[14]

Diebenkorn's colleague at CSFA, David Park, similarly grappled with the preeminence of nonobjective painting in postwar American art. In an act of artistic rebellion, in late 1949 or early 1950 Park inaugurated the Bay Area Figurative movement when he discarded all his Abstract Expressionist canvases at the Berkeley dump and boldly shifted to painting in a representational mode (pl. 32). Park was followed by several Bay Area artists (including Diebenkorn, Elmer Bischoff, and later Joan Brown and Roland Petersen) in reconciling the gestural brushwork of Abstract Expressionism with figurative subjects (pls. 31, 33, and 34).[15]

Diebenkorn returned to working in a predominantly nonrepresentational mode after moving to Los Angeles in 1966. In the luminous, streamlined compositions in his Ocean Park series, which he produced while renting a studio in the eponymous neighborhood of Santa Monica, Diebenkorn evoked the distinctive light and gridlike geometries of his urban environs (pl. 30). Such tensions between representation and abstraction are also evident in the enigmatic, hard-edged paintings of Southern California artist Helen Lundeberg, and in the nature-based compositions of artists working in the Bay Area such as Bernice Bing, Jay DeFeo, and Yu-ho Tseng (pls. 27, 28, 35, and 36).

In the 1950s, in response to the perceived soullessness, consumerism, and conformism of postwar American life, counterculture movements emerged in California, and their philosophies and aesthetic influences are reflected in the work of Beat artists such as Bruce Conner, DeFeo, George Herms, and Jess. In the following decade, fueled by opposition to America's involvement in the Vietnam War, gatherings such as the 1967 Summer of Love put San Francisco on the map as the birthplace of the hippie movement, which permeated the culture of college campuses

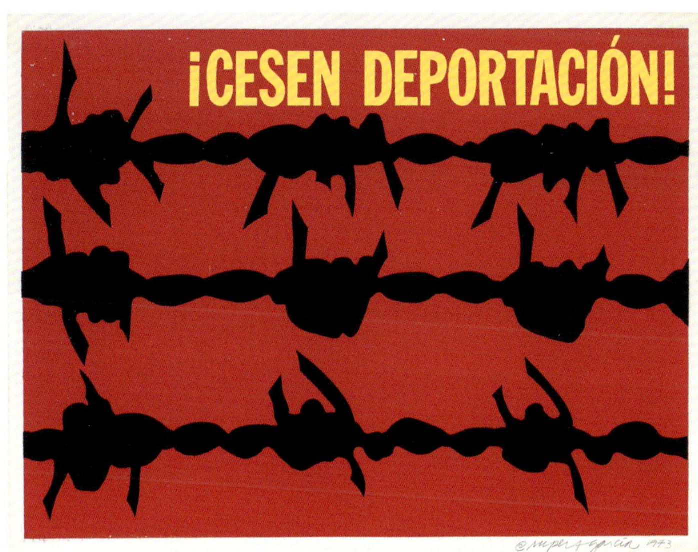

9 | Rupert Garcia (b. 1941), *¡Cesen Deportación!*, 1973. Color screenprint, 18 11/16 x 25 1/8 in. (47.5 x 63.8 cm). Gift of Mr. and Mrs. Robert Marcus, 1990.1.111

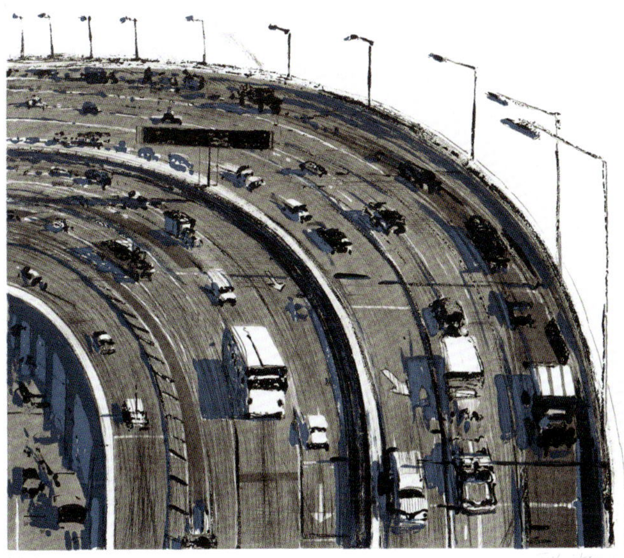

10 | Wayne Thiebaud (1920–2021), Parasol Press Ltd. (active 20th century), publisher, *Freeway Curve*, 1979. Color drypoint and aquatint, 18 7/8 x 22 in. (47.8 x 55.8 cm). Crown Point Press Archive, museum purchase, Achenbach Foundation for Graphic Arts Endowment Fund, 1991.28.269

in California and beyond (fig. 8). Simultaneously, activists associated with the Chicano, Black Power, gay liberation, feminist, and other civil rights movements protested the nation's subjugation of people of color, members of LGBTQ+ communities, and women. Many artists working during this era addressed California's own shameful legacy of racism — which includes the genocide of Native Americans; the forced internment of people of Japanese ancestry during World War II; and the exclusion, marginalization, and exploitation of the region's Black, Asian, and Latin American laborers and residents (fig. 9).

Environmental concerns also rose to the fore in the postwar era. Once celebrated for its natural beauty, the California landscape was increasingly perceived as tarnished and impoverished by rapacious resource consumption and overdevelopment. Some contemporary artists overtly depicted the ravages of natural disasters, many of which have been exacerbated by human actions (pls. 45 and 46), or of corrupt or harmful farming practices. Others more subtly reflected or critiqued the impacts of human encroachment on the landscape. In *Freeway Curve* (1979), Wayne Thiebaud captured the prosaic realities of traffic congestion, and the seemingly endless stretches of freeways in late twentieth-century California (fig. 10). In *Four Palm Trees* (1969), Robert Bechtle wryly explored the banality and artificiality of the suburban landscape, deploying his characteristic Photorealist precision to depict a sparsely planted group of palm trees silhouetted against a distant, low-lying group of tract homes (pl. 41).[16]

Adopting a similarly deadpan style, in *A Particular Kind of Heaven* (1983/2005) Ed Ruscha evoked the romanticized

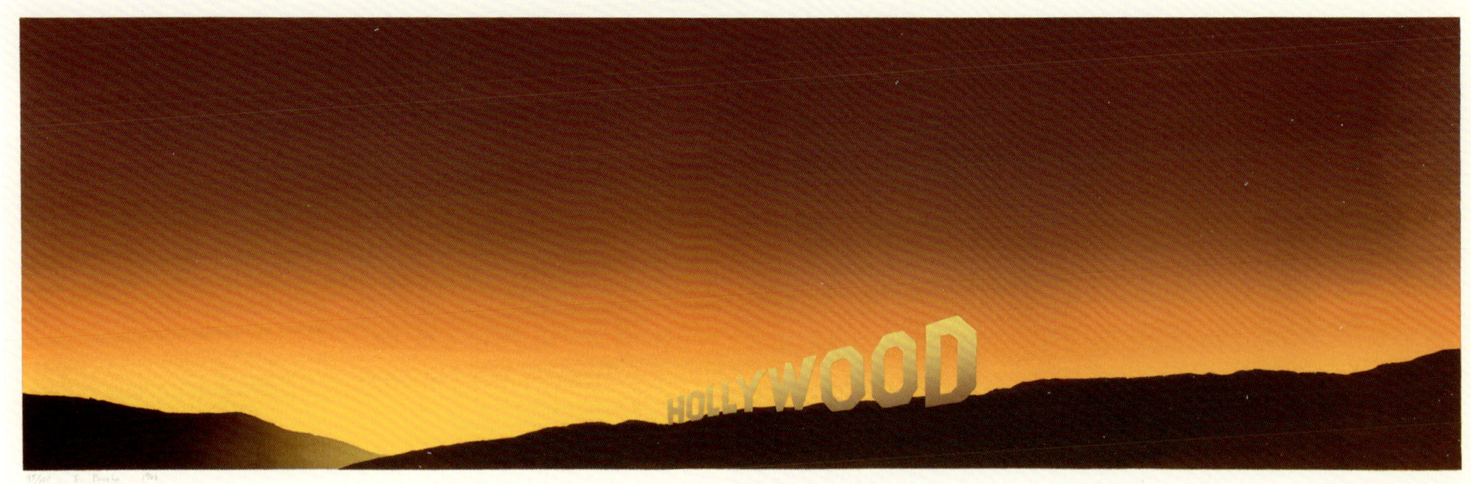

11 | Ed Ruscha (b. 1937), *Hollywood*, 1968. Screenprint, 17 ½ x 44 7⁄16 in. (44.5 x 112.9 cm). Museum purchase, Mrs. Paul L. Wattis Fund, 2000.131.7.1

representations of landscape found in classic western films to convey the popular perception of California as a mythical El Dorado (pl. 50). Recalling a film title projected on a flat movie screen, the large-scale triptych features white capital letters that resemble those in the iconic Los Angeles HOLLYWOOD sign, a recurrent motif in Ruscha's work (fig. 11). In *Fog over San Quentin State Prison, San Quentin, California* (2001), Sandow Birk referenced and subverted the symbolic visual rhetoric of earlier artistic traditions such as the Hudson River School (pl. 49). The composition derives from a nineteenth-century coastal New England scene by John Frederick Kensett (1816–1872), but Birk's inclusion of a distant view of the state's oldest prison grimly alludes to California's shockingly high incarceration rate.[17]

The work of Richard Mayhew also highlights the continuity between earlier American landscape traditions and contemporary American art. In *Rhapsody* (2002), Mayhew's vivid, animating color harmonies refer to American Tonalism, while also incorporating the influences of Abstract Expressionism, jazz, and the artist's African American and Native American heritage (pl. 6). Mayhew's joyful, and highly personal, expression of his experience of nature affirms the enduring and restorative splendor of the California landscape, which despite decades of human intervention remains a potent source of mental, physical, spiritual, and artistic rejuvenation.

California's abundant natural resources and breathtaking landscapes have for millennia sustained human life, elicited reverence, and sparked creativity. Yet in more recent history they have been harnessed and consumed by an ever-expanding population, intensifying California's inherent susceptibility to extreme weather conditions and natural disasters. Despite reports of destructive earthquakes, wildfires, and drought, as well as housing shortages and widening income inequality, the California Dream persists, fueling countless migrations to this western frontier from within and outside the borders of the United States. Whether seeking economic advancement, social liberation, or artistic inspiration, these new generations of Californians extend the region's grand tradition of pioneering change. Art produced in California reflects these contrasts, challenges, and opportunities — capturing, in a remarkable range of styles and from multiple perspectives, the tensions between the utopian idealism that has long defined the region, and the complex realities of life in the Golden State.

NOTES

1 Garci Rodríguez de Montalvo, *Las Sergas de Esplandián* (*The Adventures of Esplandián*) (ca. 1510).

2 This expedition was followed by Englishman Sir Francis Drake's possible 1579 landing in Drake's Bay near Point Reyes, the 1587 arrival of Filipino sailors in Spanish ships at Morro Bay, and Sebastián Vizcaíno's 1602 mapping of the California coast for New Spain.

3 Terming their enterprise the "Sacred Expedition," in 1769–1770 the inspector general José de Gálvez y Gallardo, the Franciscan priest Junípero Serra y Ferrer, and the soldier and administrator Gaspar de Portolá extensively explored California's interior and cemented Spain's territorial claims to the region. Spanish military forces built several presidios, or forts, and three small pueblos, or towns, which eventually gave rise to larger cities such as Los Angeles and San Jose.

4 During the Spanish colonial period, Native Californians were devastated by the harsh conditions of mission life — including forced relocation and conversion to Christianity, enslavement, and exposure to diseases such as measles and diphtheria — and their population declined by over thirty percent under Spanish and subsequently Mexican (1821–1846) rule. During Mexico's governance of California, the missions were secularized and land grants were distributed to native-born and naturalized Mexican citizens. Despite being marked by instability, conflict, and the continued oppression of Native Californians by the newly powerful rancheros, this period was sentimentalized by later generations of artists and writers, such as Helen Hunt Jackson, author of the popular 1884 novel *Ramona*.

5 Albert Bierstadt's *View of Donner Lake, California* (1871–1872) is based on sketches the artist made of the scenery he witnessed from the comfort of a train car while traveling across the Sierra Nevada mountain range in 1871. See Nancy Anderson, "'The Kiss of Enterprise': The Western Landscape as Symbol and Resource," in *The West as America: Reinterpreting Images of the Frontier, 1820–1920*, ed. William Truettner (Washington, DC, and London: Smithsonian Institution Press, 1991), pp. 237–283.

6 As Richard Rodriguez writes, "In 1849, Chilean and Scot and Chinese and Aussie and Mexican and Yankee — people of every age and tongue and disused occupation — waded knee-deep through the mud of Amador County." Rodriguez, "Where the Poppies Grow," in *Made in California: Art, Image, and Identity, 1900–2000* (Berkeley: University of California Press, 2001), p. 273.

7 See Timothy Anglin Burgard, "Charles Christian Nahl, From the Prairie to the Parlor," in Timothy Anglin Burgard et al., *Masterworks of American Painting at the de Young* (San Francisco: Fine Arts Museums of San Francisco, 2005), pp. 94–97.

8 Bierstadt traveled to California four times; on his second trip in 1871 he stayed in San Francisco for two years and three months. *California Spring* was painted in Bierstadt's New York studio in 1875, based on sketches completed during his 1871 trip to San Francisco.

9 Construction of the state capitol building was completed only a year before Bierstadt finished the painting.

10 Teikichi Hikoyama's painting was inspired by the fictitious story of "The Sleeping Maiden" featured in Dan Totheroh's 1921 Mountain Play, *Tamalpa*, in which Mount Tamalpais assumes the recumbent form of a lovestruck woman who sacrificed herself on the slopes of the mountain.

11 Chiura Obata disseminated his aesthetic philosophy to Bay Area audiences as a teacher and practitioner of the modern *nihonga* (Japanese-style painting) movement.

12 Diego Rivera visited San Francisco three times in the 1930s, producing the murals *Allegory of California* (1931) at the Pacific Stock Exchange Club, *The Making of a Fresco, Showing the Building of a City* (1931) at the San Francisco Art Institute, and *Pan-American Unity* (1940) for the Golden Gate International Exposition. The twenty-five muralists responsible for the twenty-seven frescos in San Francisco's Coit Tower (1933–1934) were disciples or admirers of Rivera, and depicted "Aspects of Life in California, 1934" in a Social Realist style that expressed their sympathies for the region's working classes.

13 Richard Diebenkorn enrolled in a master of fine arts program at the University of New Mexico in 1950 using funds from the GI Bill.

14 CSFA was at the time a center for Abstract Expressionism on the West Coast, with faculty including Elmer Bischoff, Edward Corbett, David Park, Mark Rothko, Hassel Smith, Clay Edgar Spohn, and Clyfford Still.

15 At the time, David Park's rejection of nonobjective painting was viewed by many in the art world as a radical defection.

16 This plant species was imported to California beginning in the eighteenth century.

17 The painting is John Frederick Kensett's *Beach at Beverly* (ca. 1869–1872). Per the Prison Policy Initiative, "California has an incarceration rate of 549 per 100,000 people (including prisons, jails, immigration detention, and juvenile justice facilities), meaning that it locks up a higher percentage of its people than many wealthy democracies do." California Profile, Prison Policy Initiative, prisonpolicy.org/profiles/CA.html, accessed March 31, 2023.

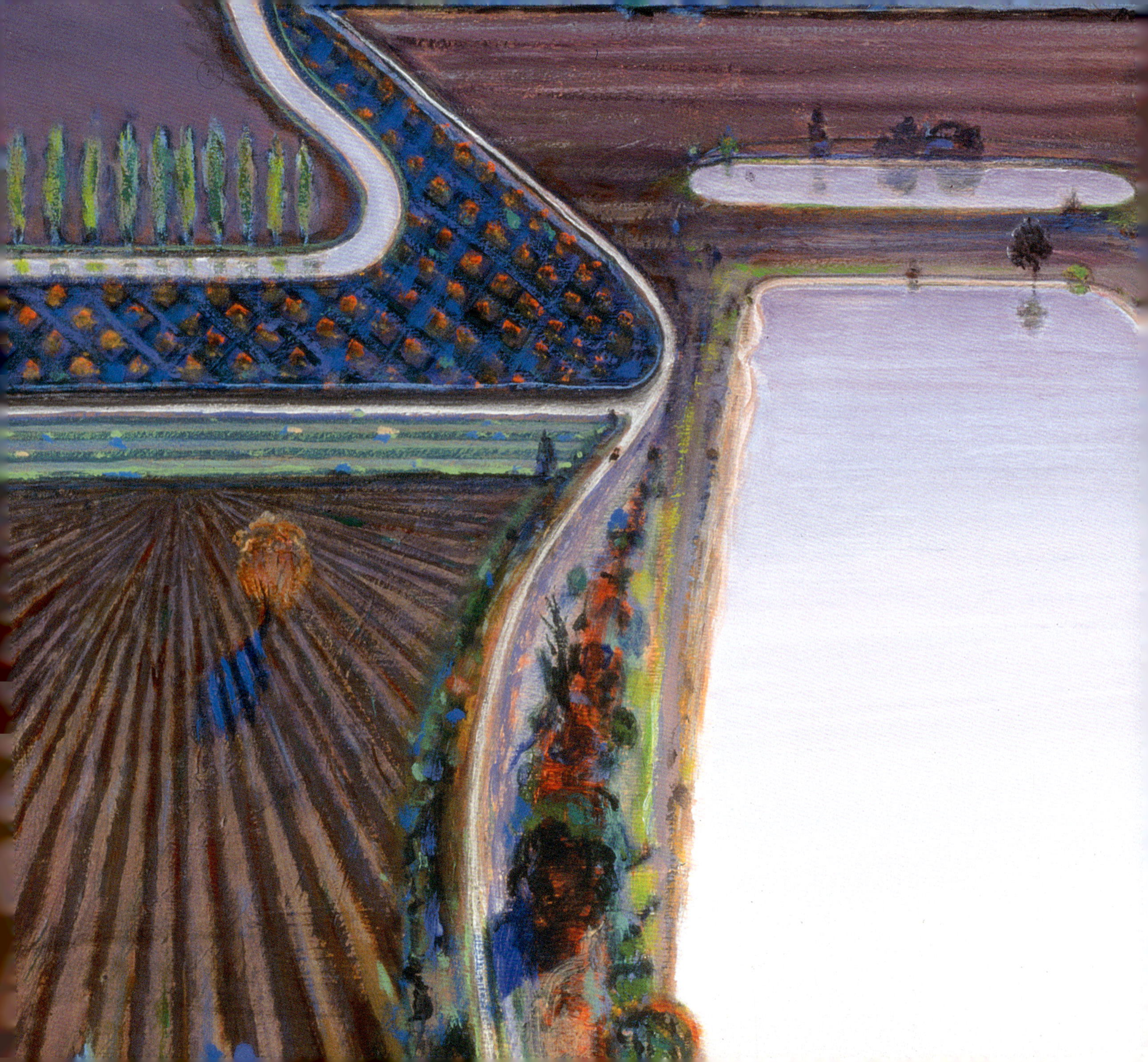

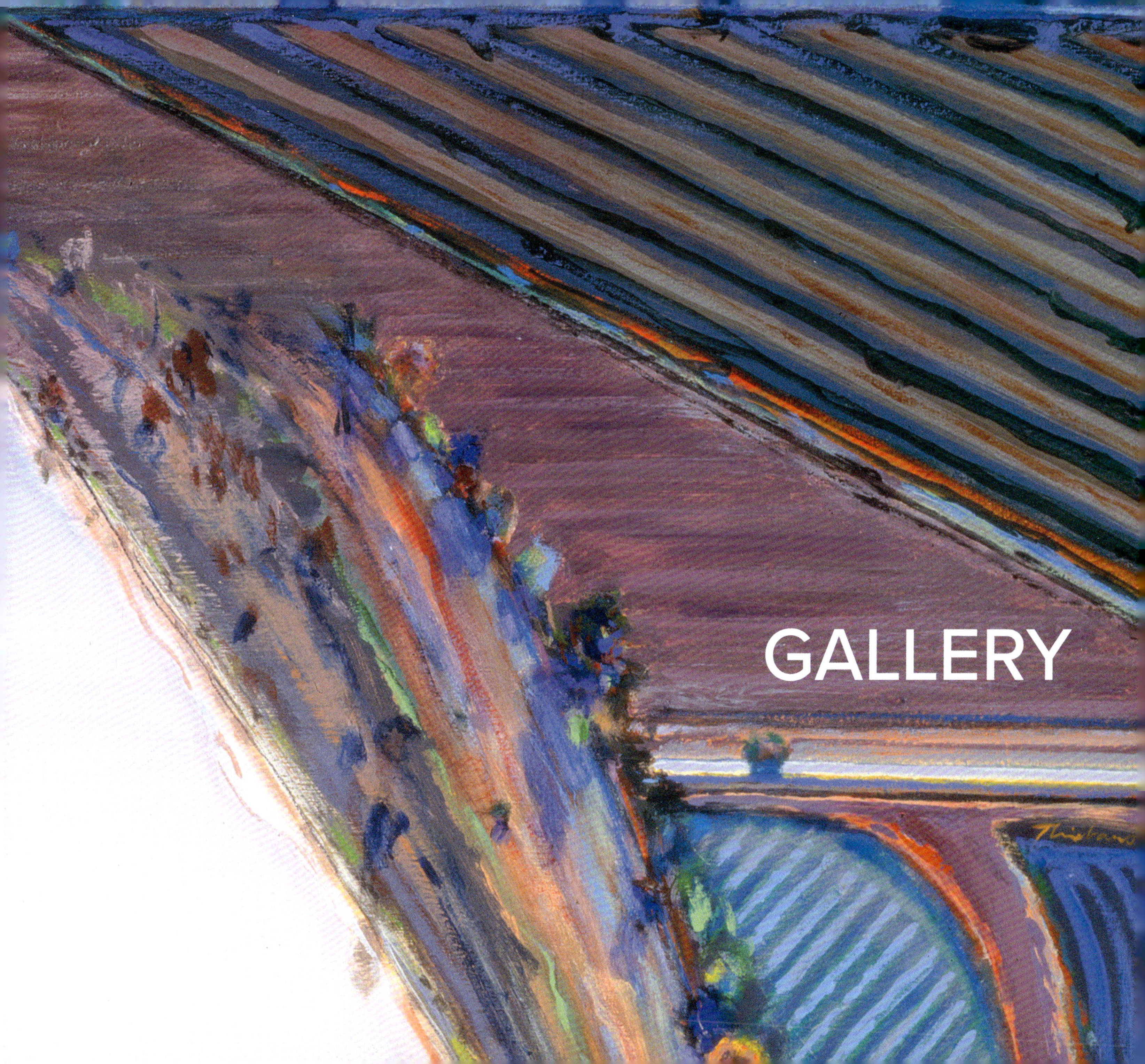

GALLERY

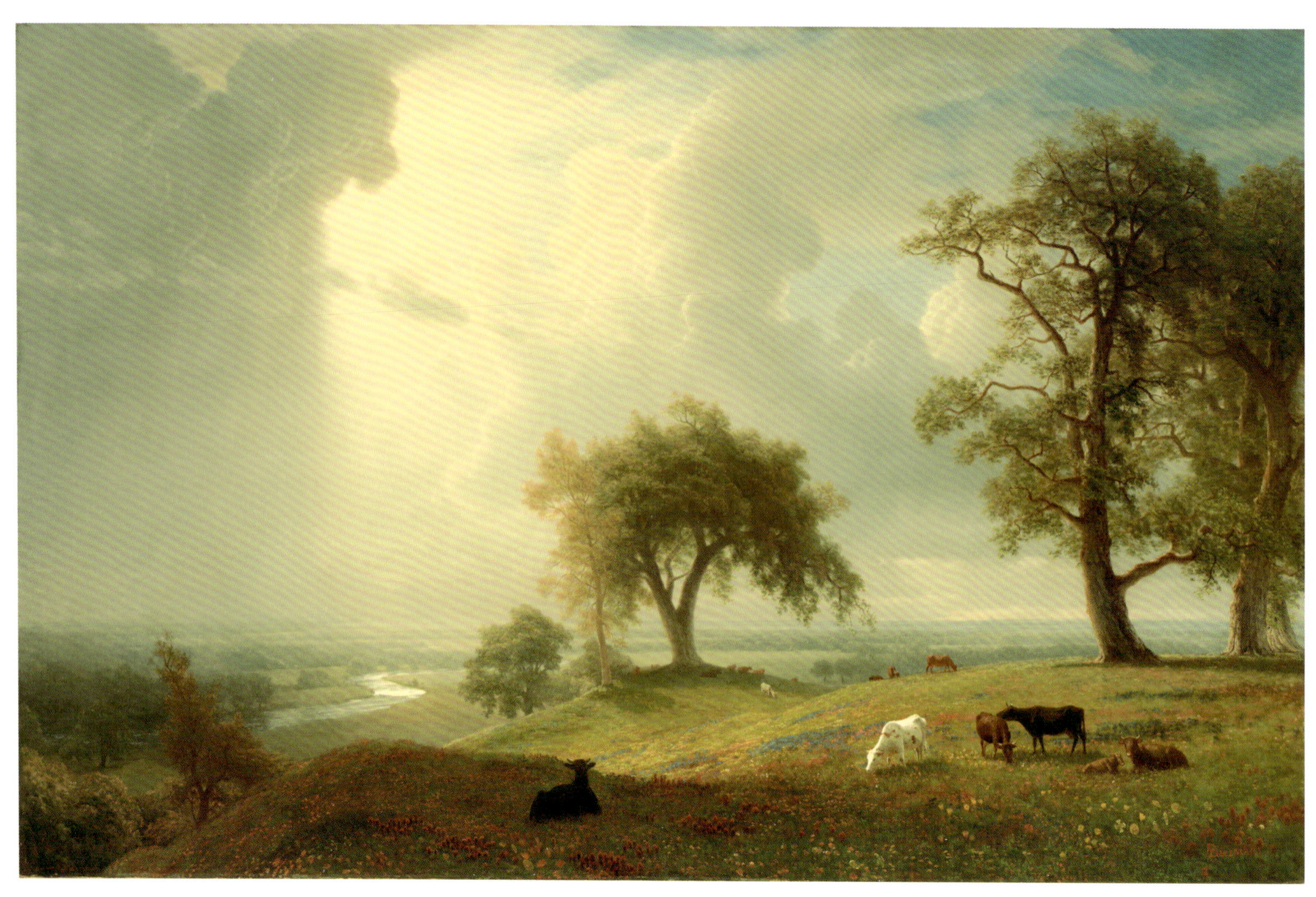

1. Albert Bierstadt (1830–1902), *California Spring*, 1875

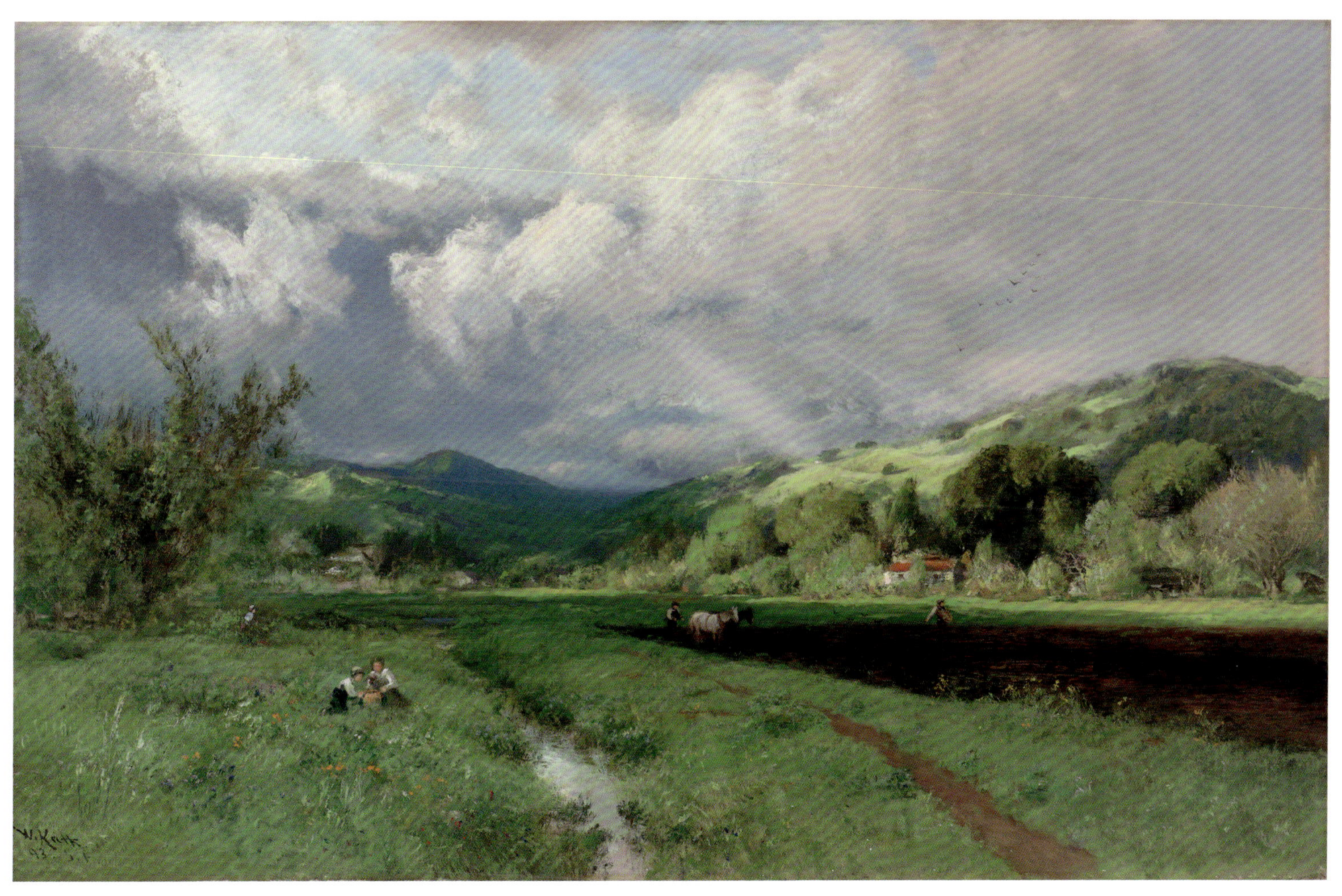

2. William Keith (1839–1911), *Spring Landscape (Spring in Marin County)*, 1893

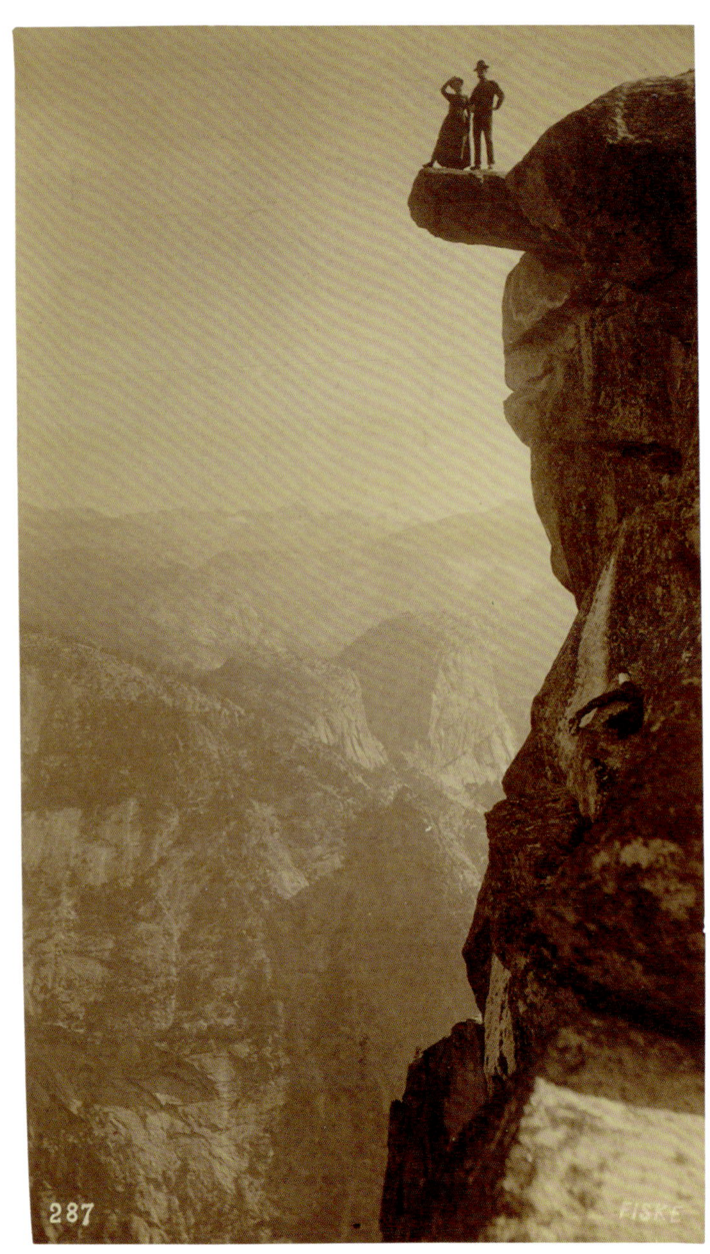

3. George Fiske (1835–1918), *Glacier Point, Yosemite*, ca. 1880

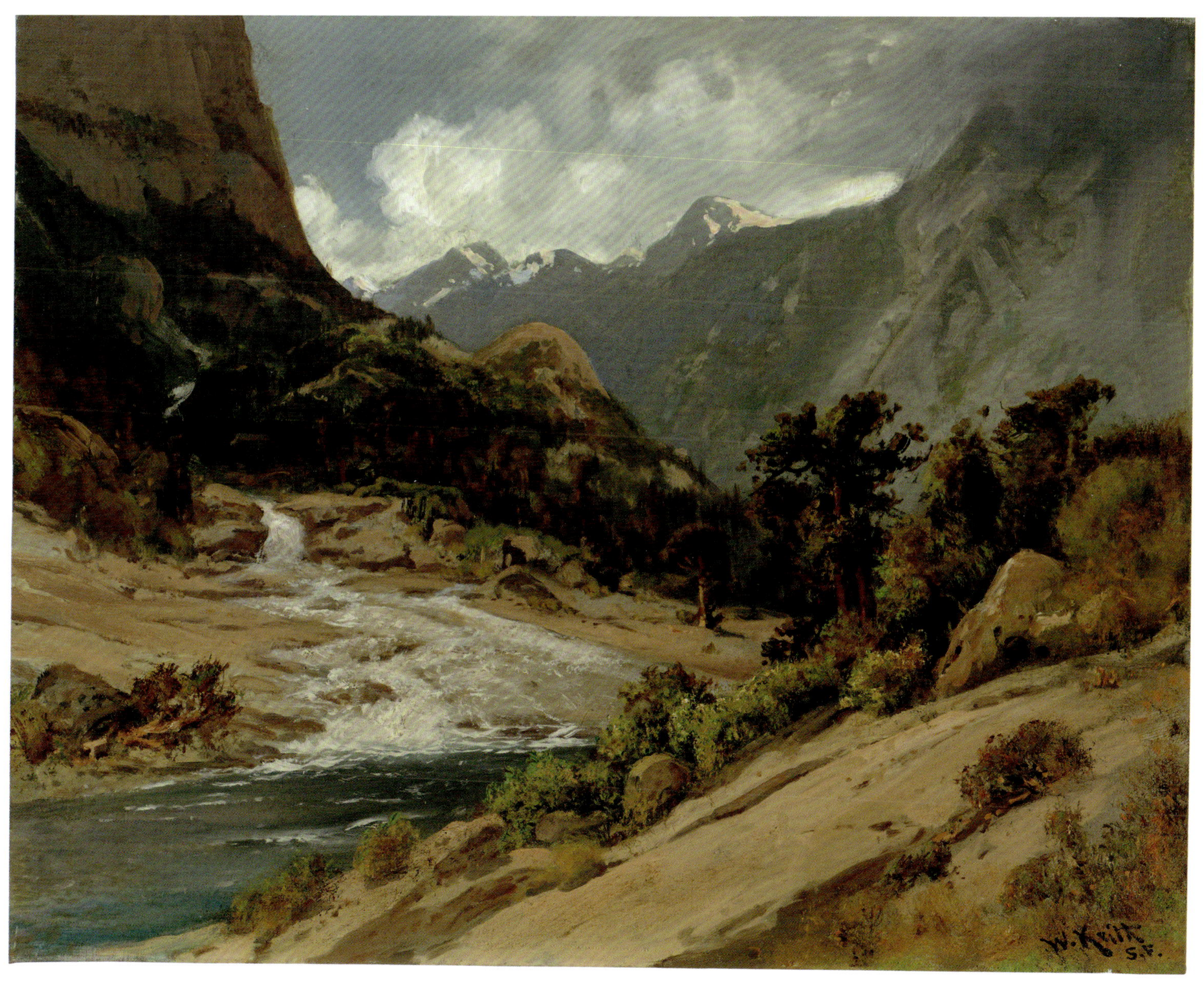

4. William Keith (1839–1911), *Hetch Hetchy Side Canyon, I,* ca. 1908

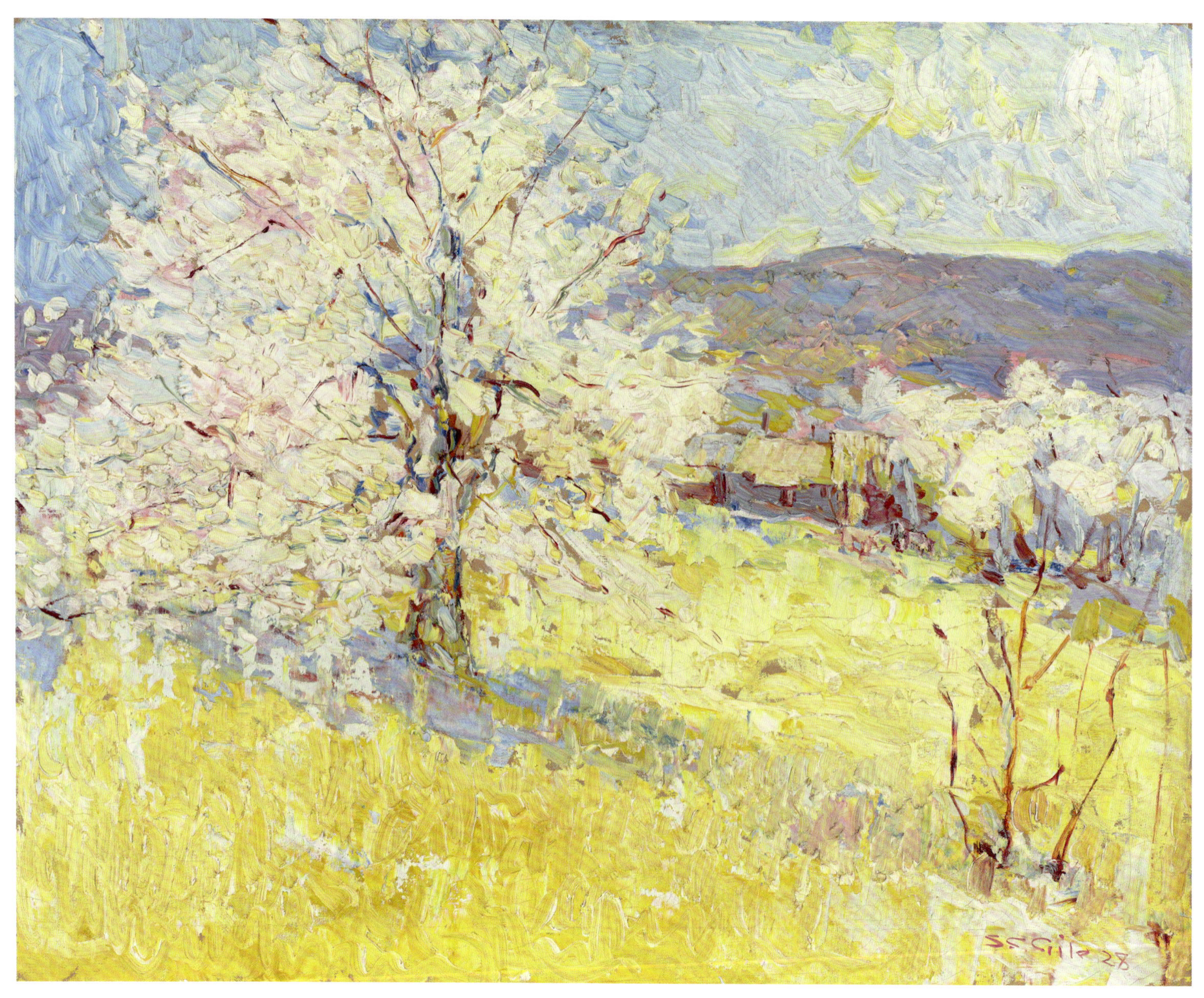

5. Selden Connor Gile (1877–1947), *Spring*, 1928

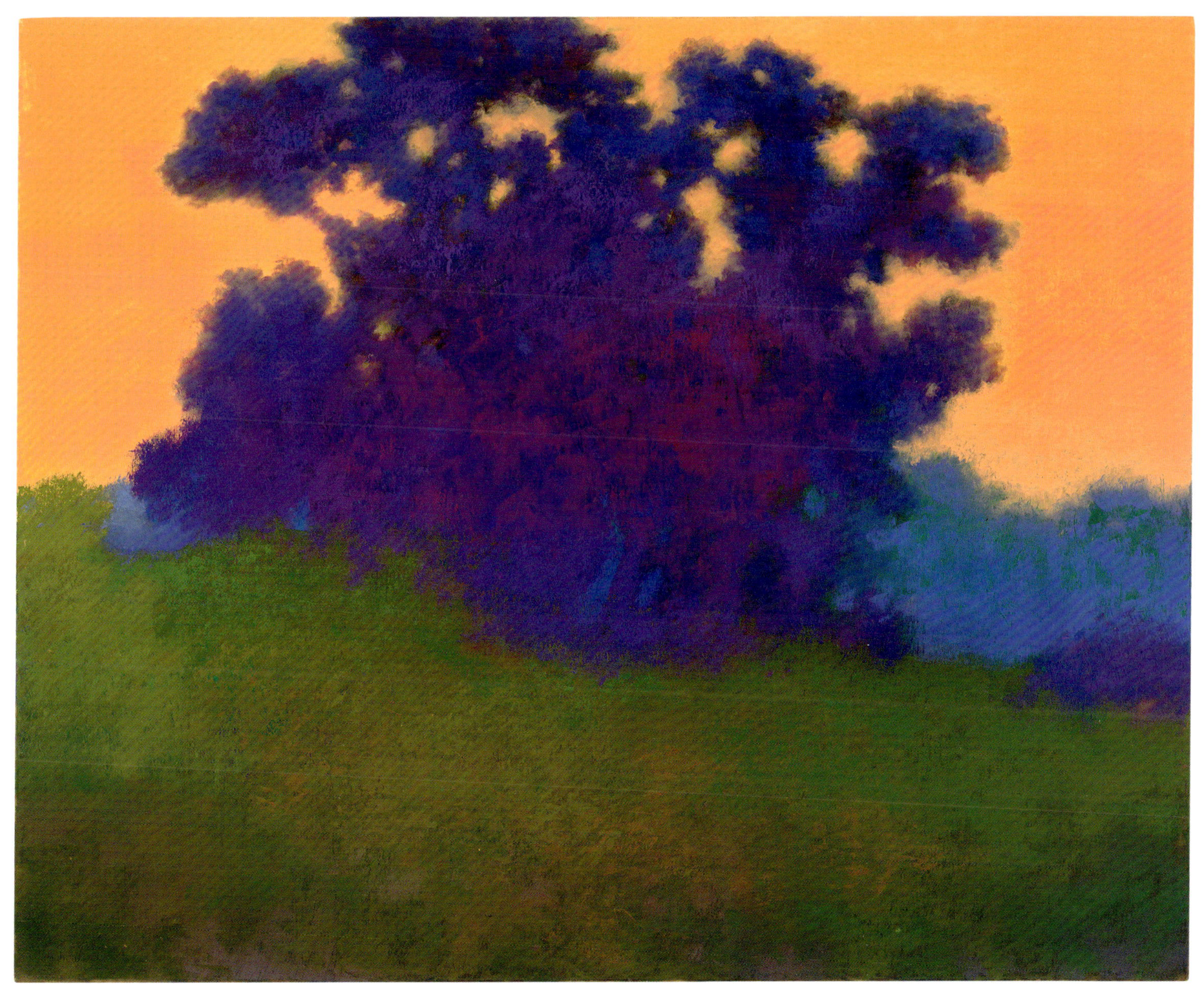

6. Richard Mayhew (b. 1924), *Rhapsody*, 2002

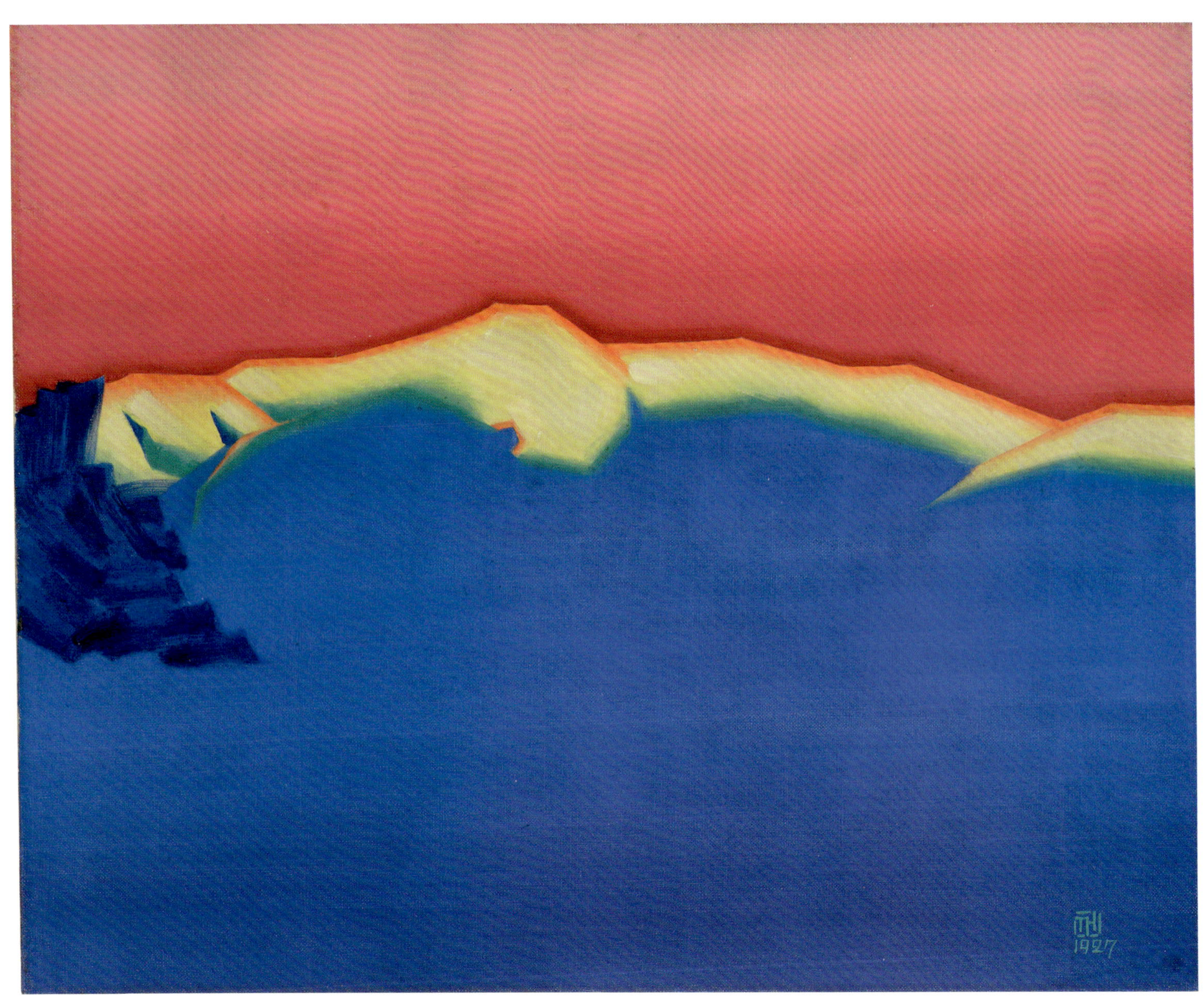

7. Teikichi Hikoyama (1884–1957), *Mt. Tamalpais*, 1927

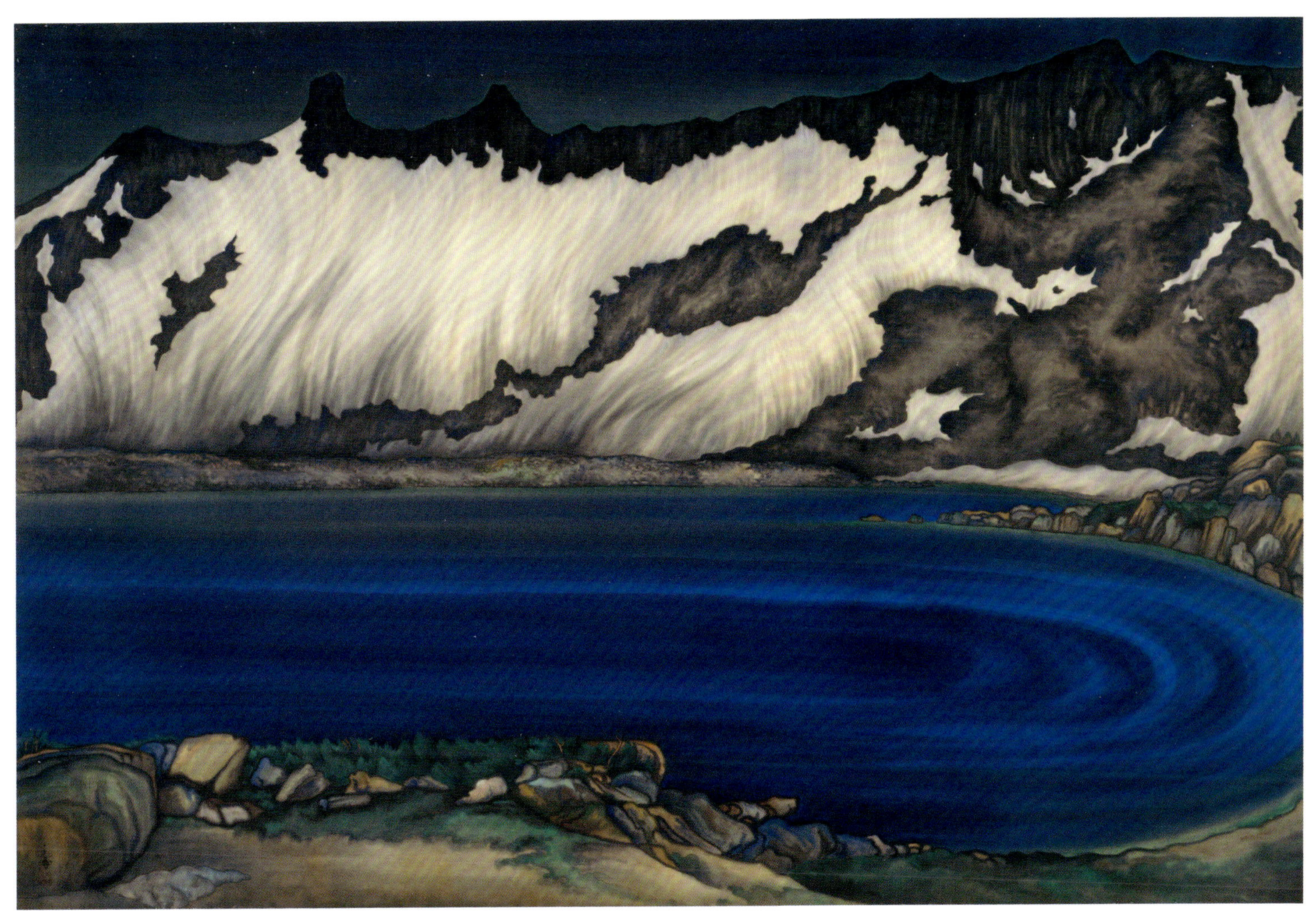

8. Chiura Obata (1885–1975), *Lake Basin in the High Sierra*, ca. 1930

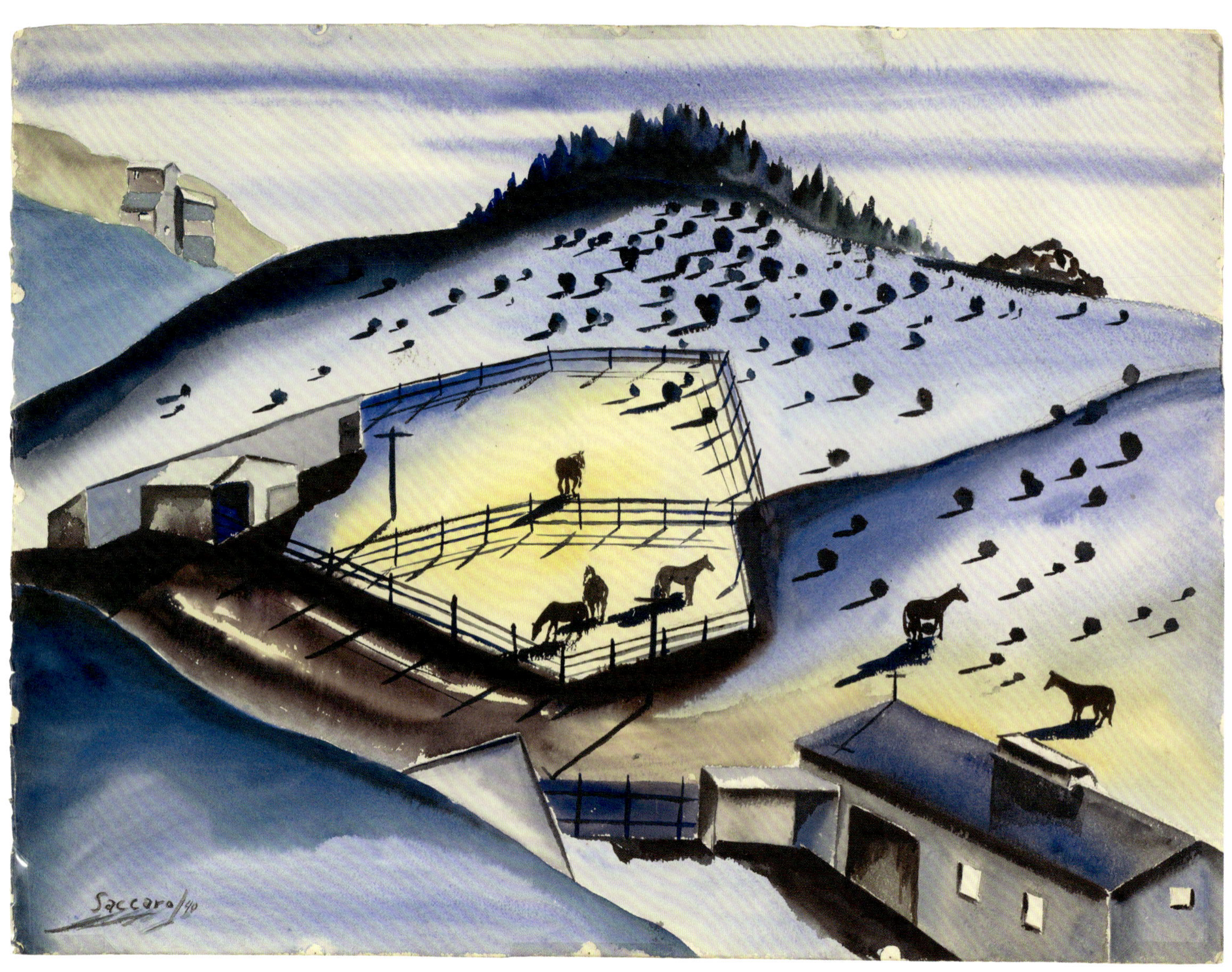

9. John Saccaro (1913–1981), *Blue Hills*, 1940

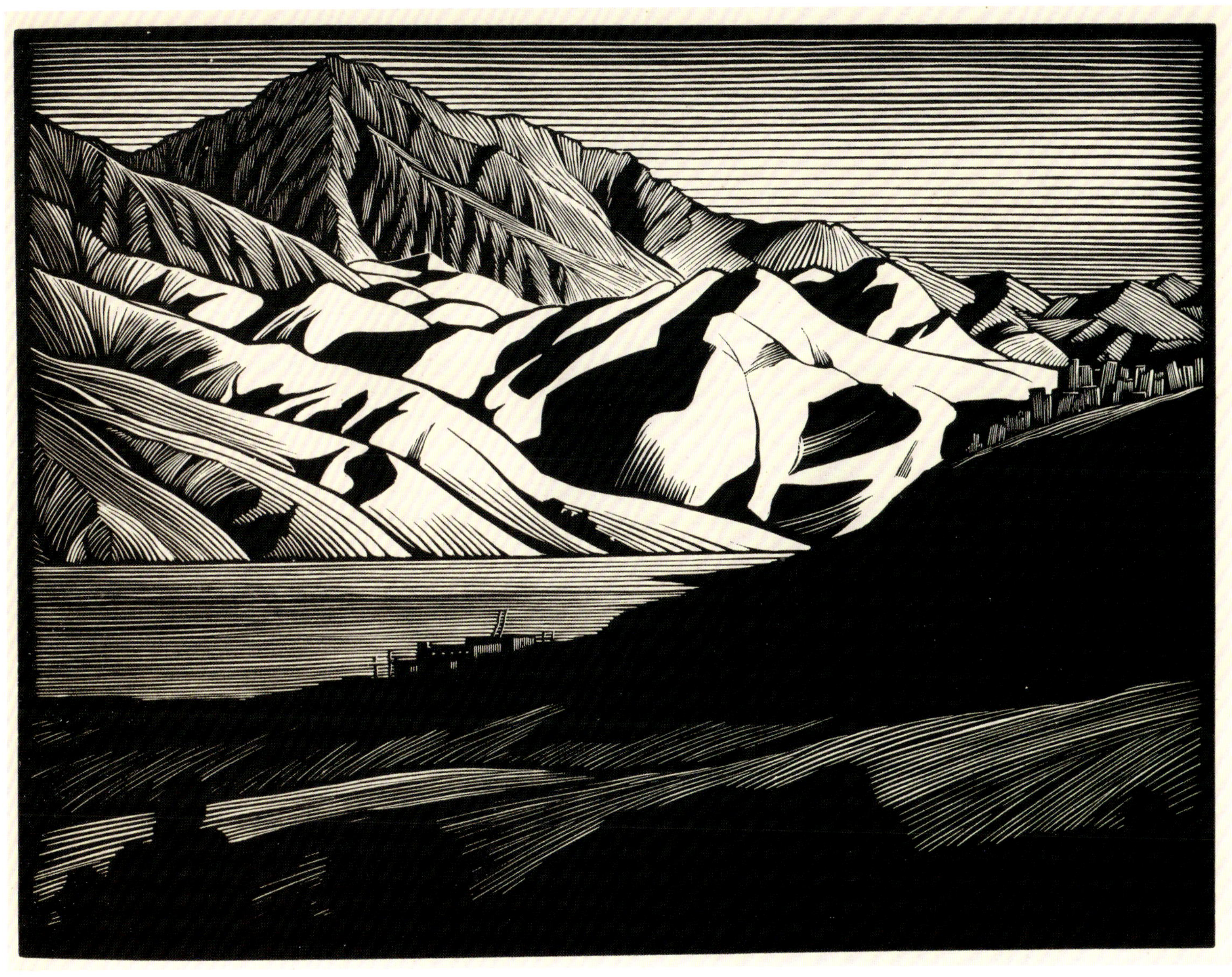

10. Paul Landacre (1893–1963), *Edge of the Desert*, plate XI in the book *California Hills and Other Wood Engravings* (Los Angeles: Bruce McCallister, 1931), 1931

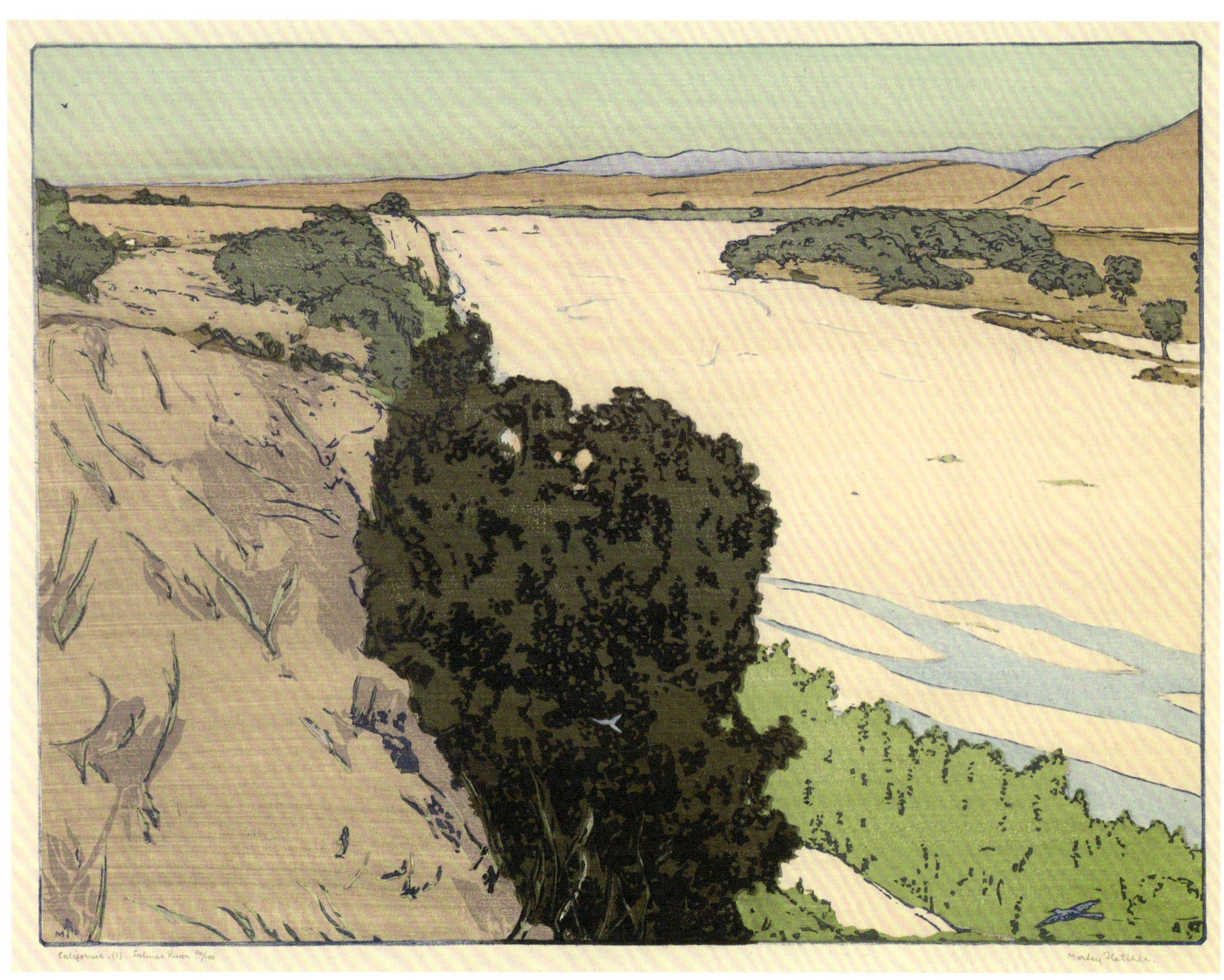

11. Frank Morley Fletcher (1866–1949), *California 1—Salinas River*, 1927–1928

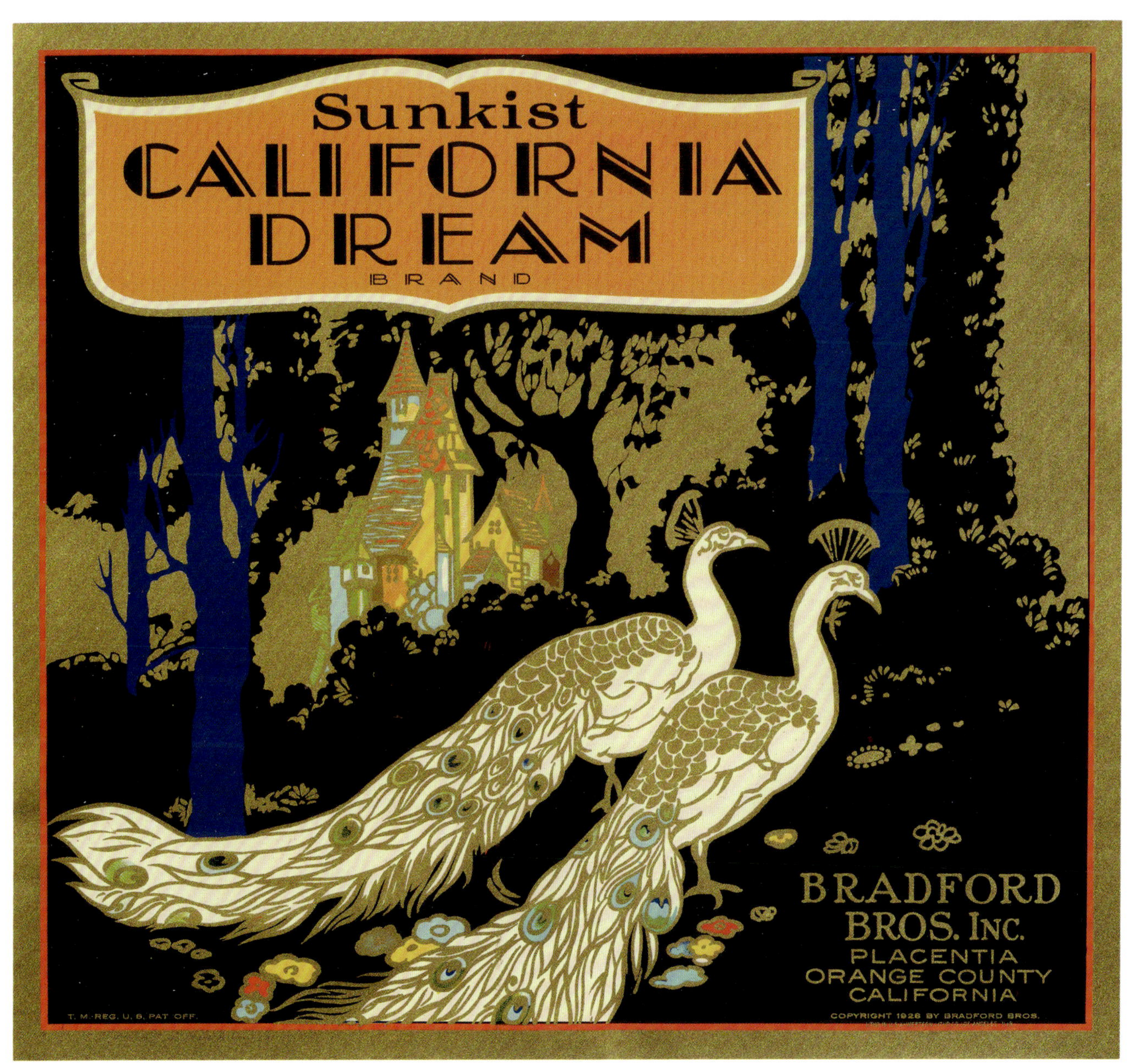

12. Unidentified artist (active 20th century), *California Dream*, ca. 1925–1940

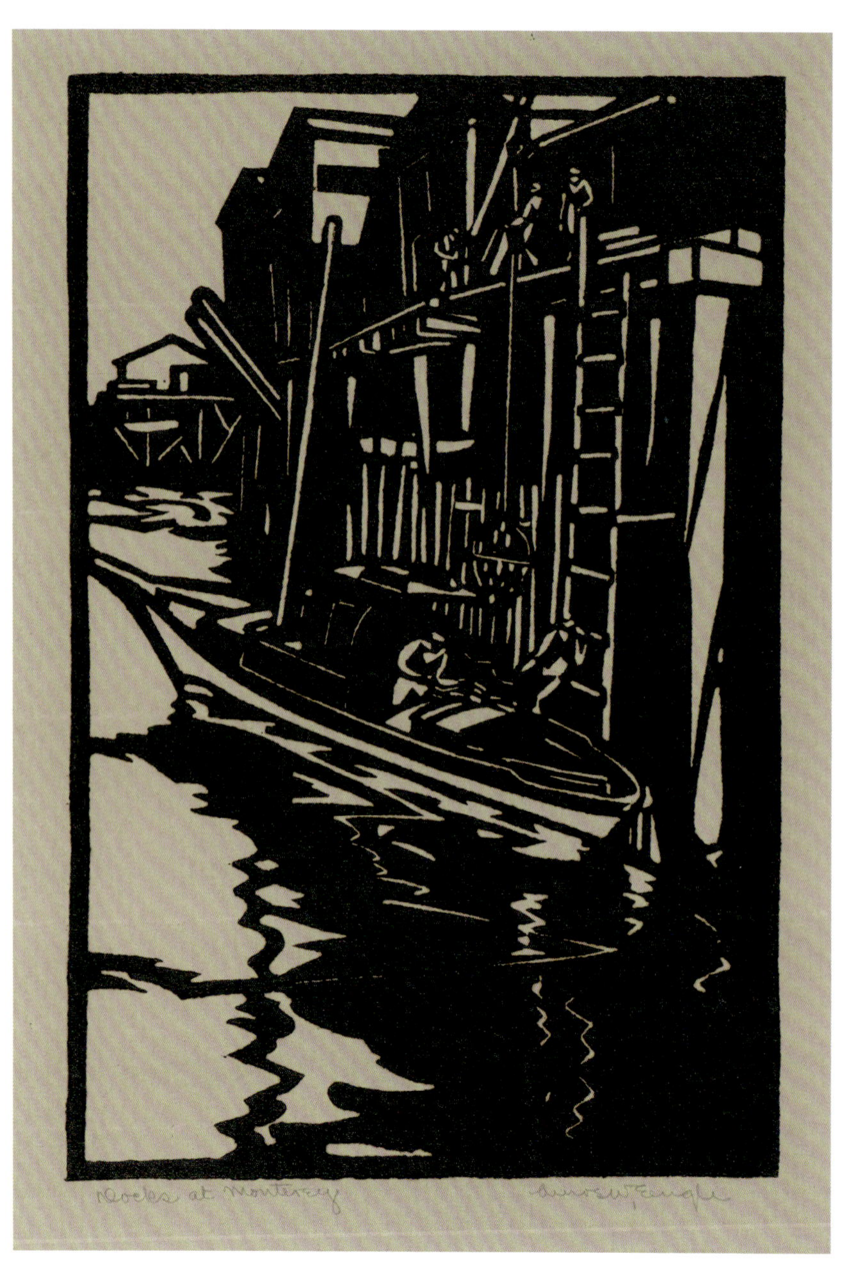

13. Amos Willis Engle (1880–1926), *Docks at Monterey*, early 20th century

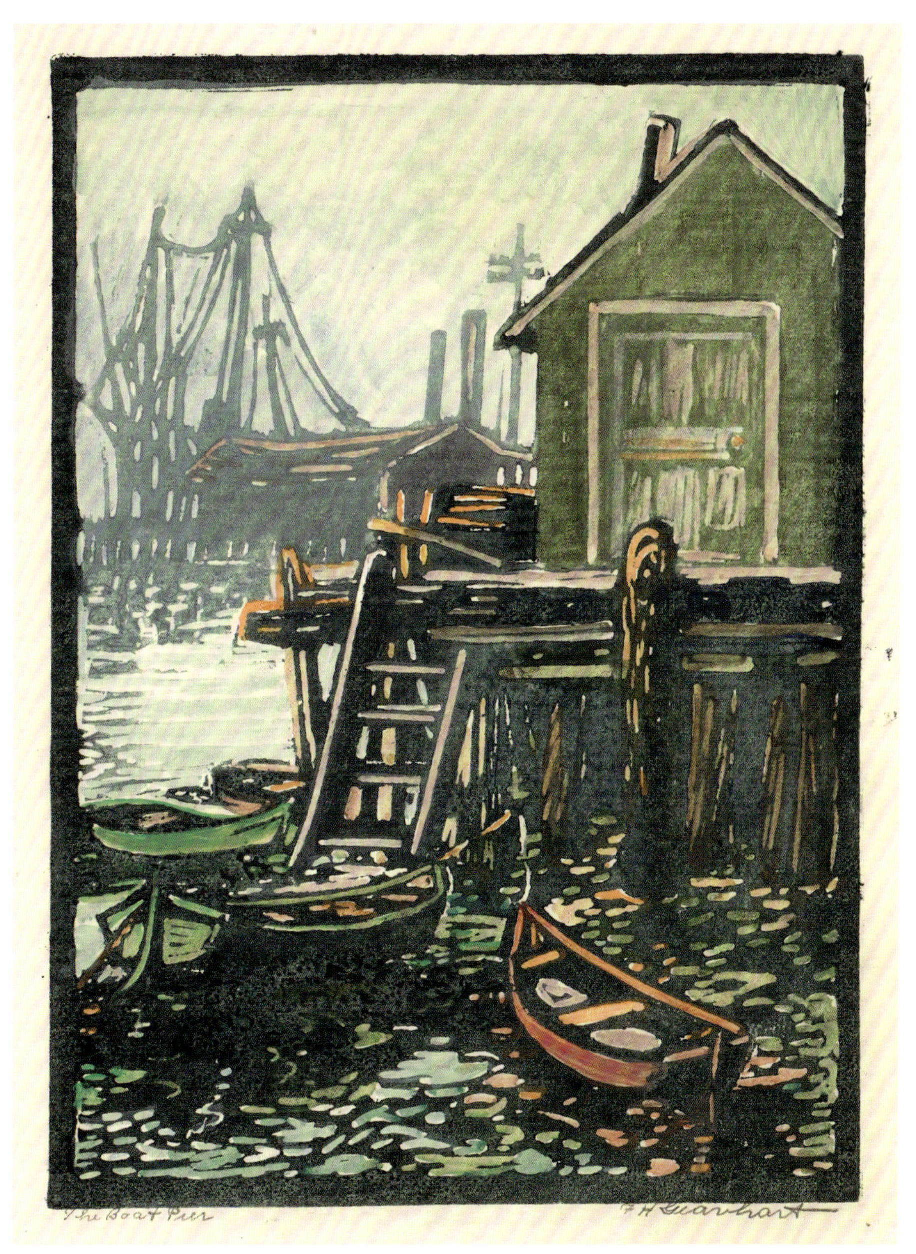

14. Frances Hammel Gearhart (1869–1958), *The Boat Pier*, 19th–20th centuries

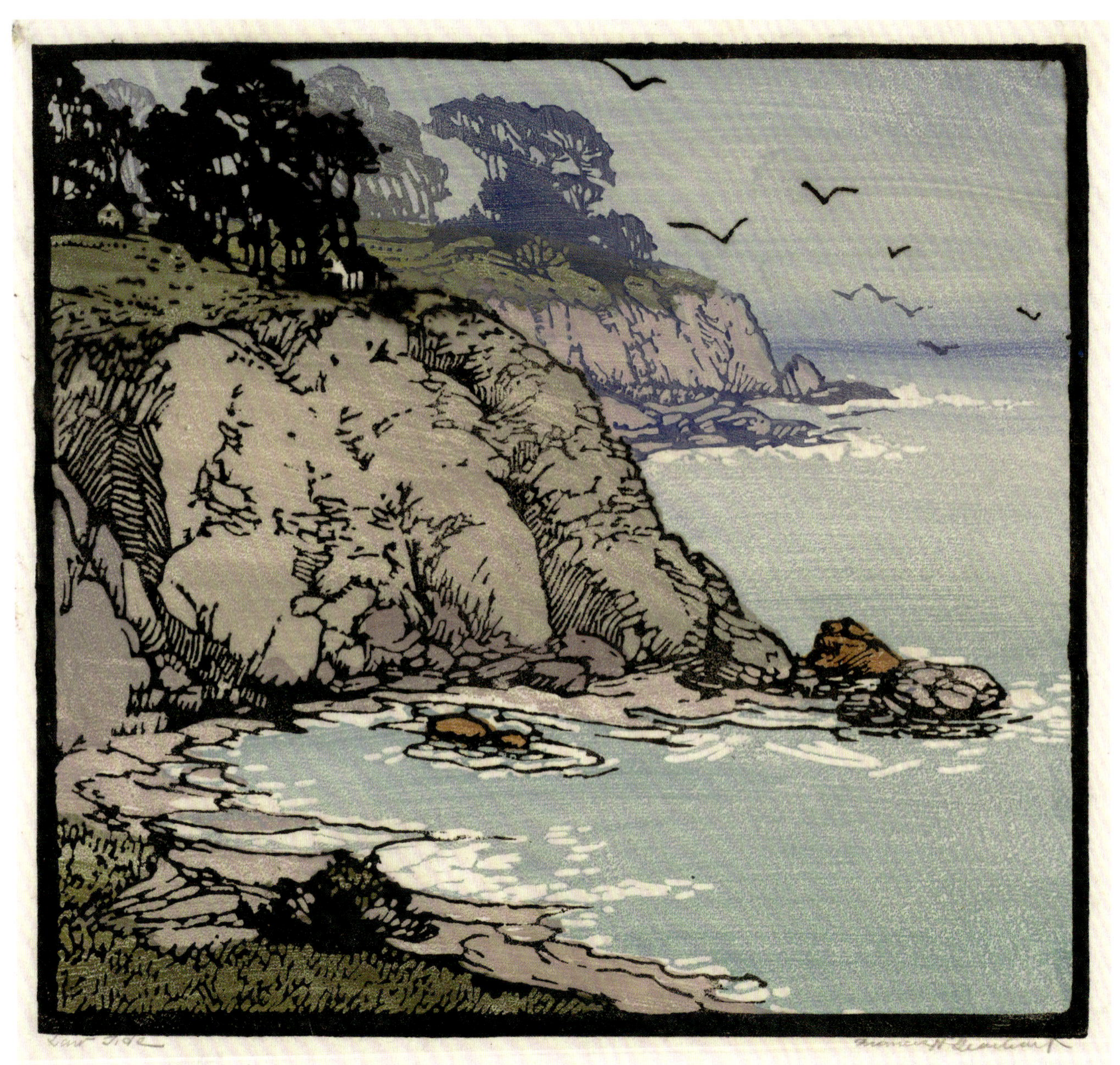

15. Frances Hammel Gearhart (1869–1958), *Low Tide*, 1930

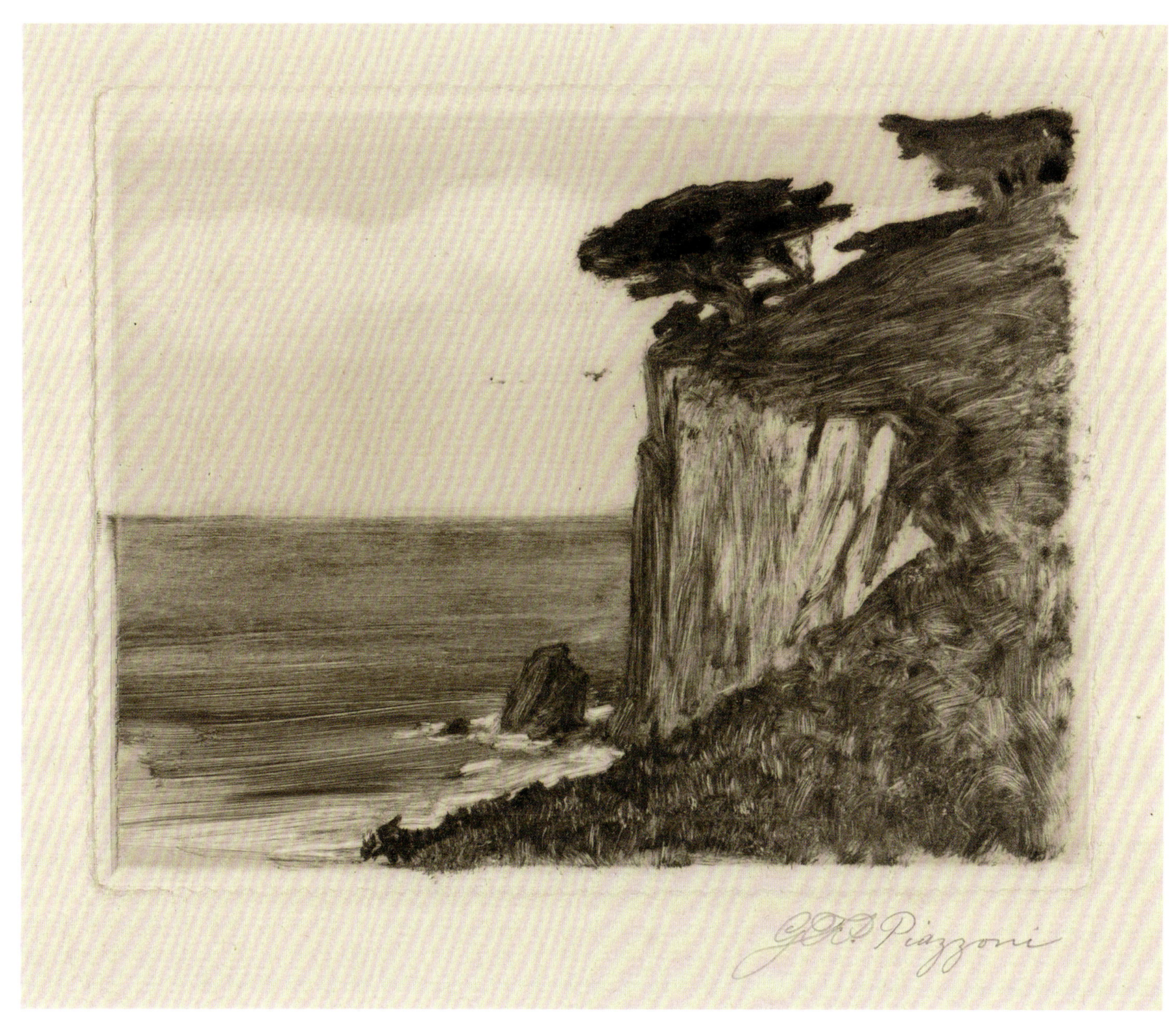

16. Gottardo Piazzoni (1872–1945), *Untitled (Seacliff and Trees)*, ca. 1910

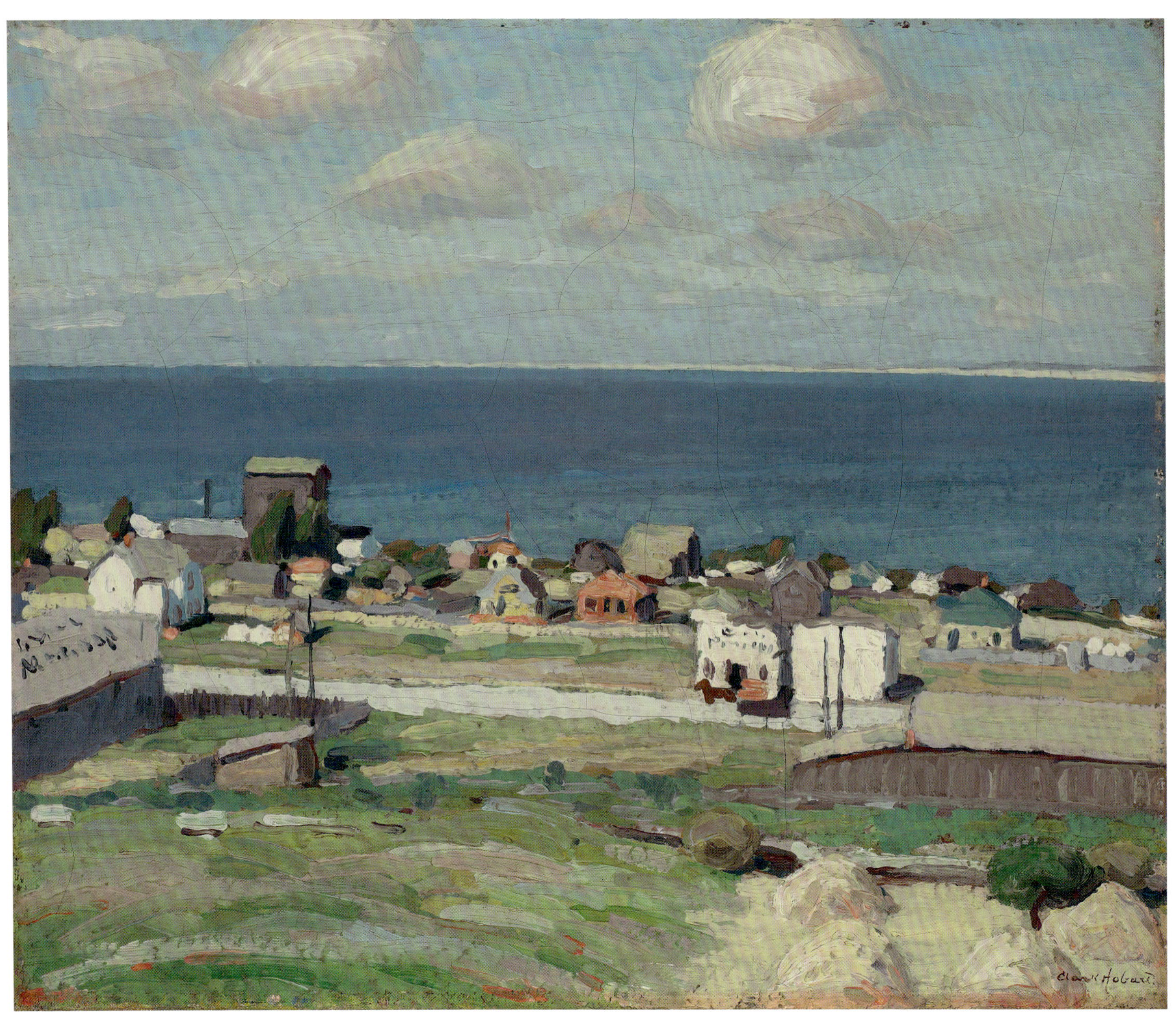

17. Clark Hobart (1868–1948), *The Blue Bay: Monterey*, ca. 1914

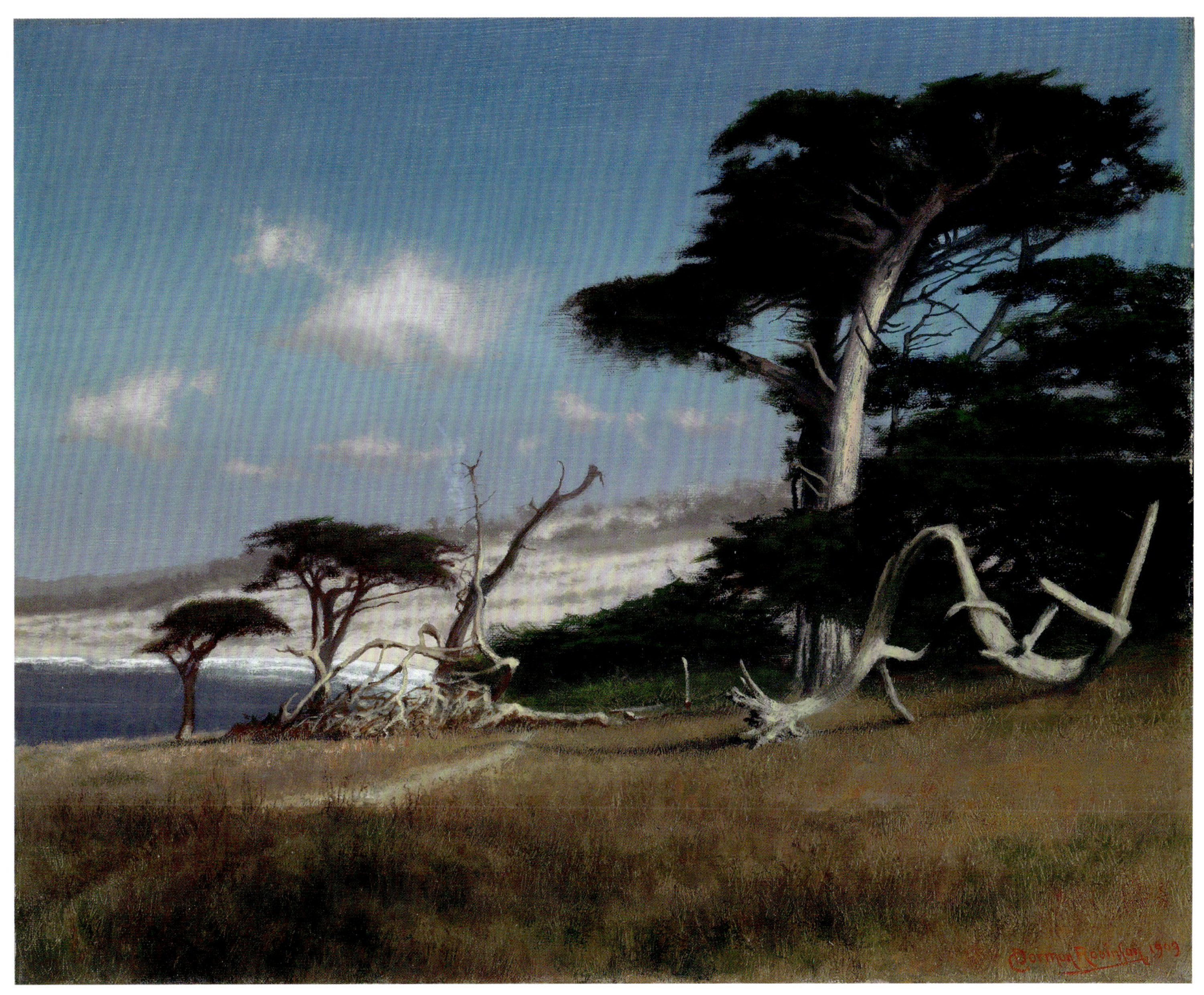

18. Charles Dorman Robinson (1847–1933), *Cypress Point, Monterey County*, 1909

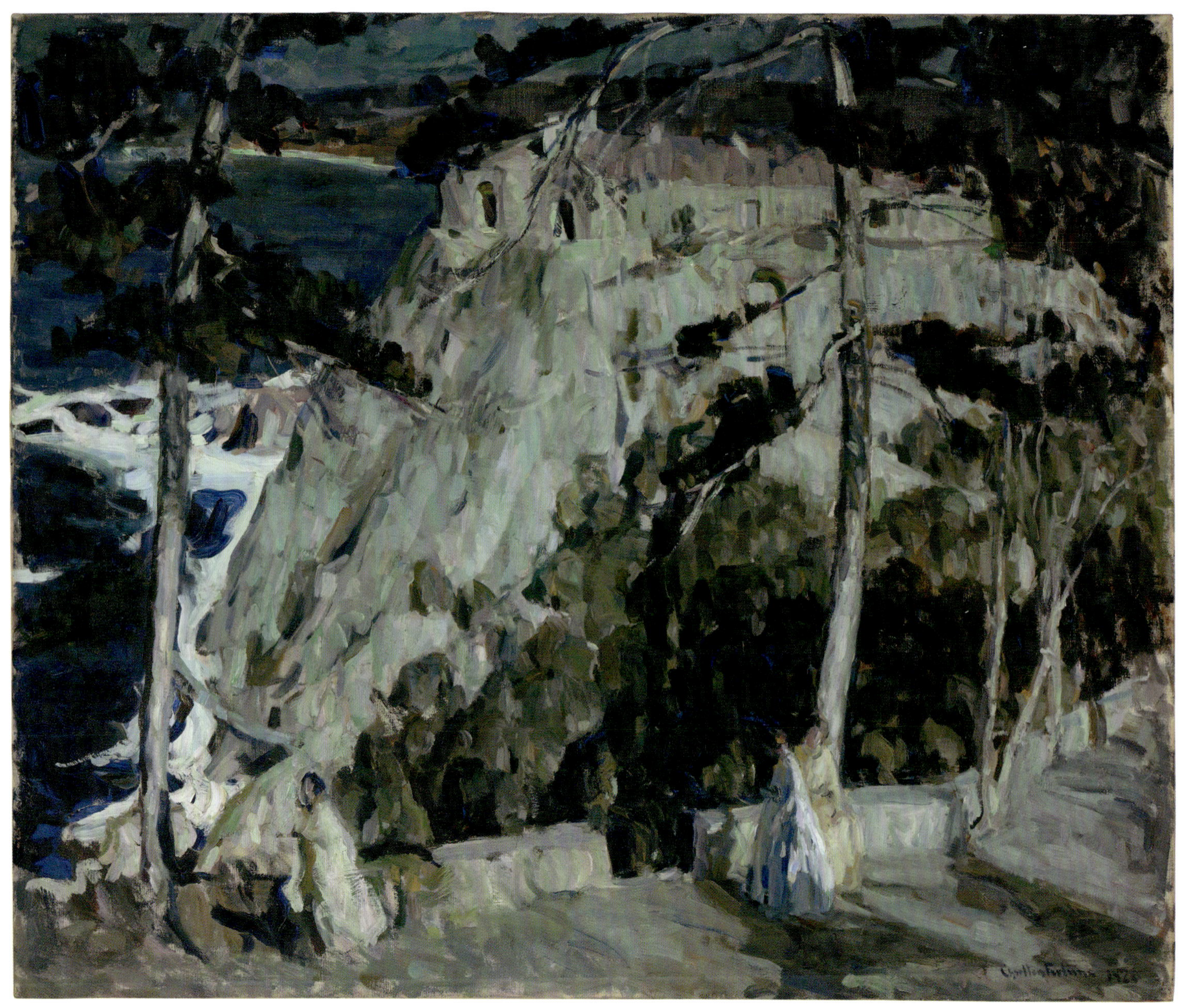

19. E. Charlton Fortune (1885–1969), *Summer Night*, 1920

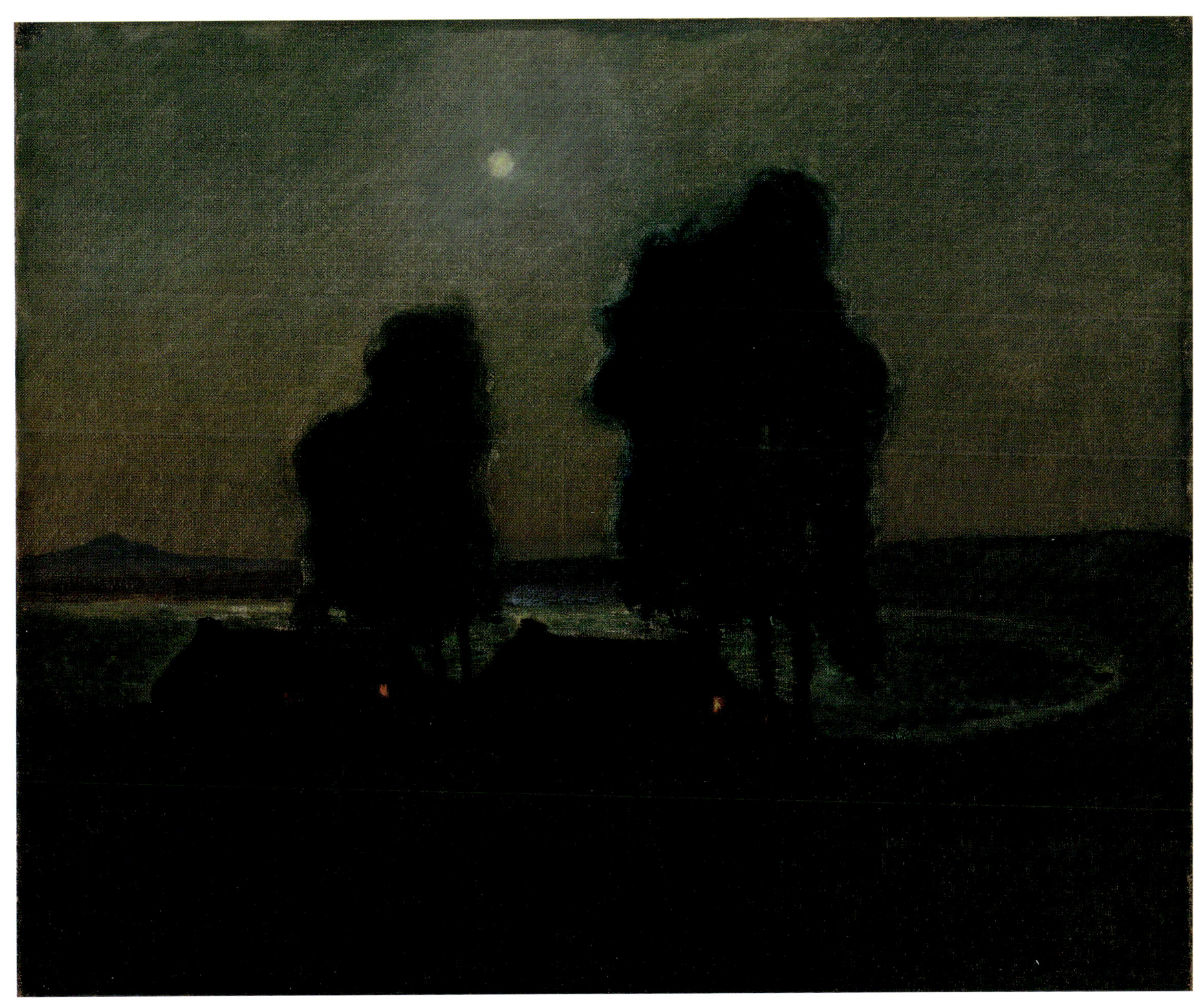

20. Charles Rollo Peters (1862–1928), *By Monterey Bay*, ca. 1895

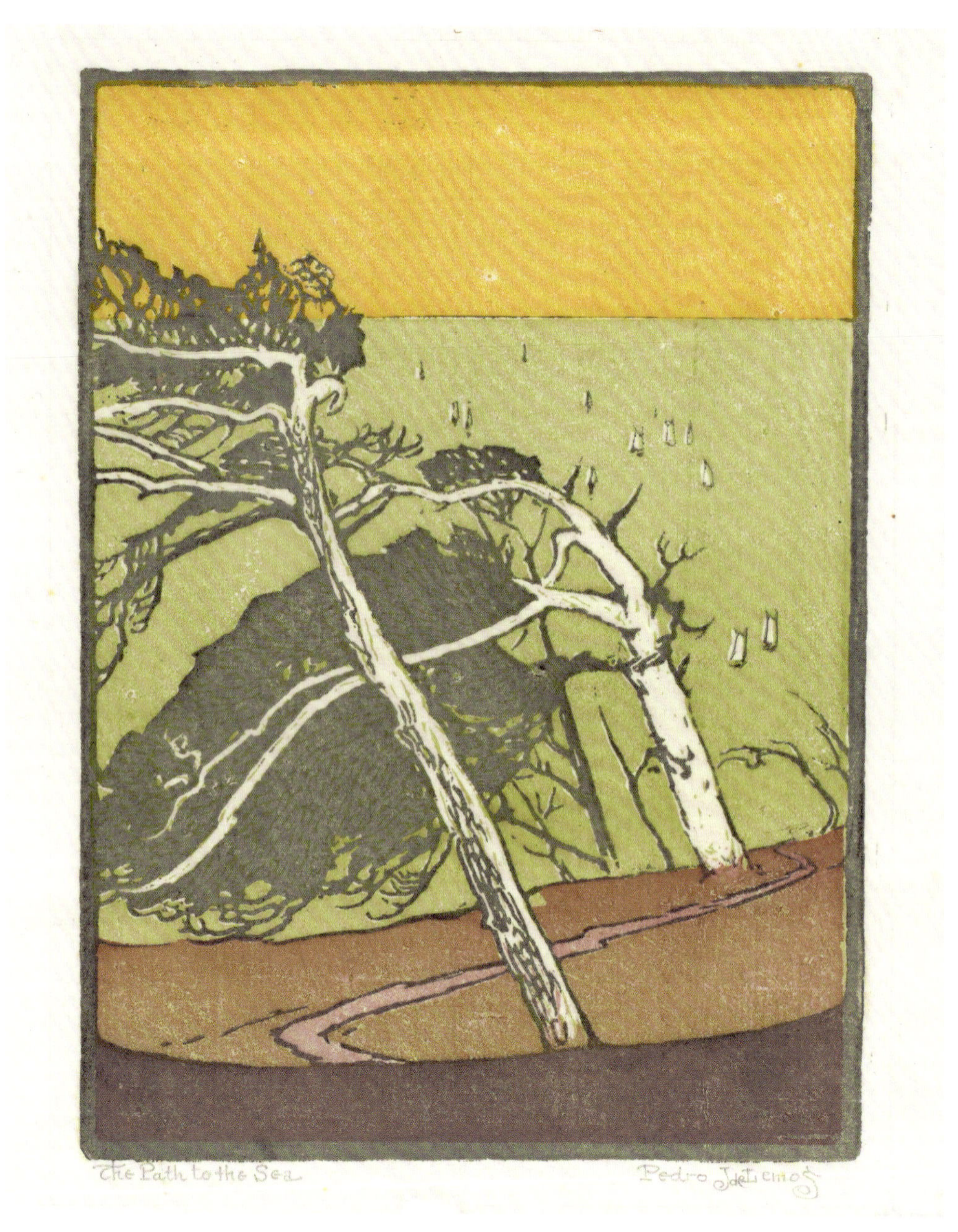

21. Pedro J. Lemos (1882–1954), *The Path to the Sea,* ca. 1915

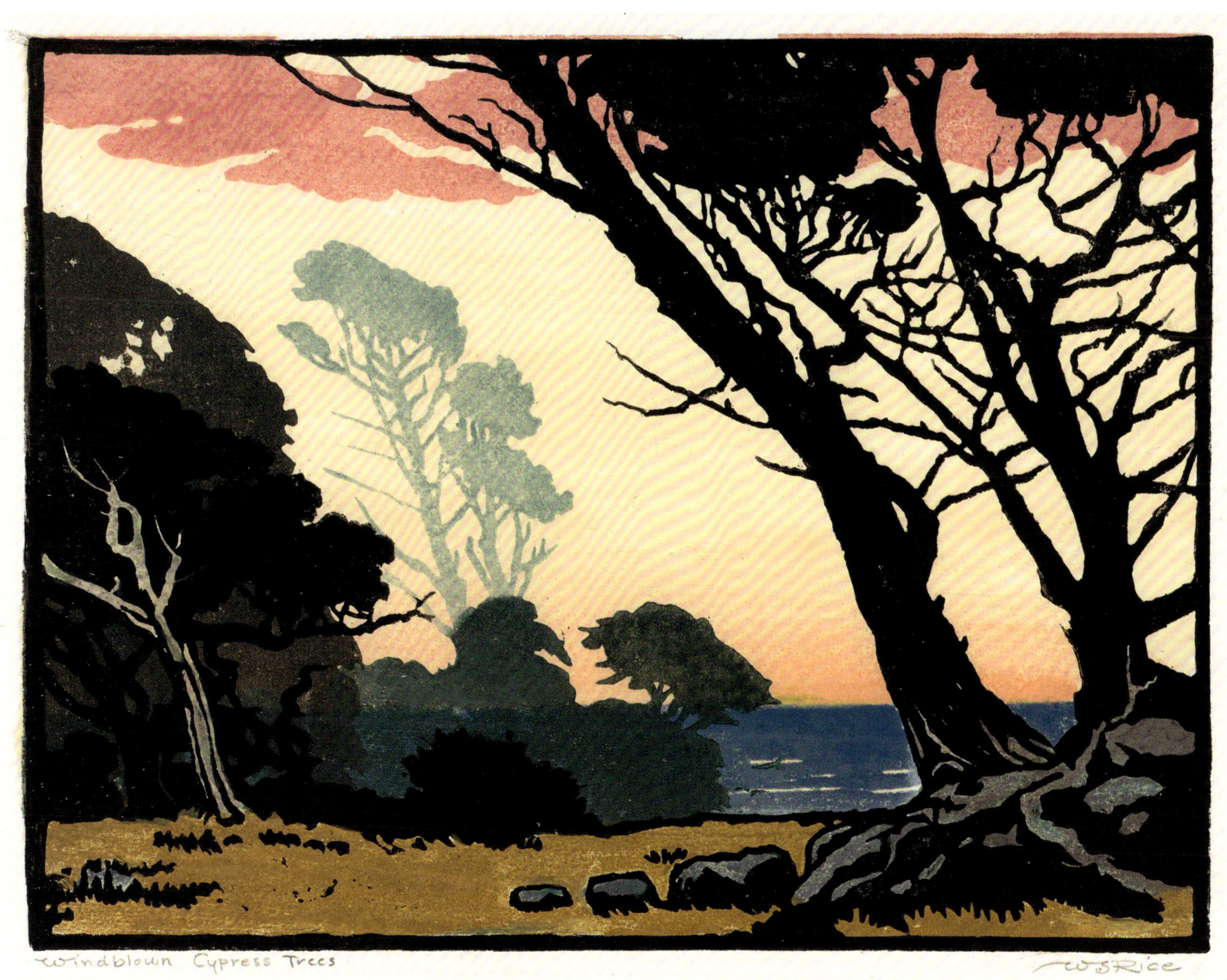

22. William Seltzer Rice (1873–1963), *Windblown Cypress Trees*, 1930

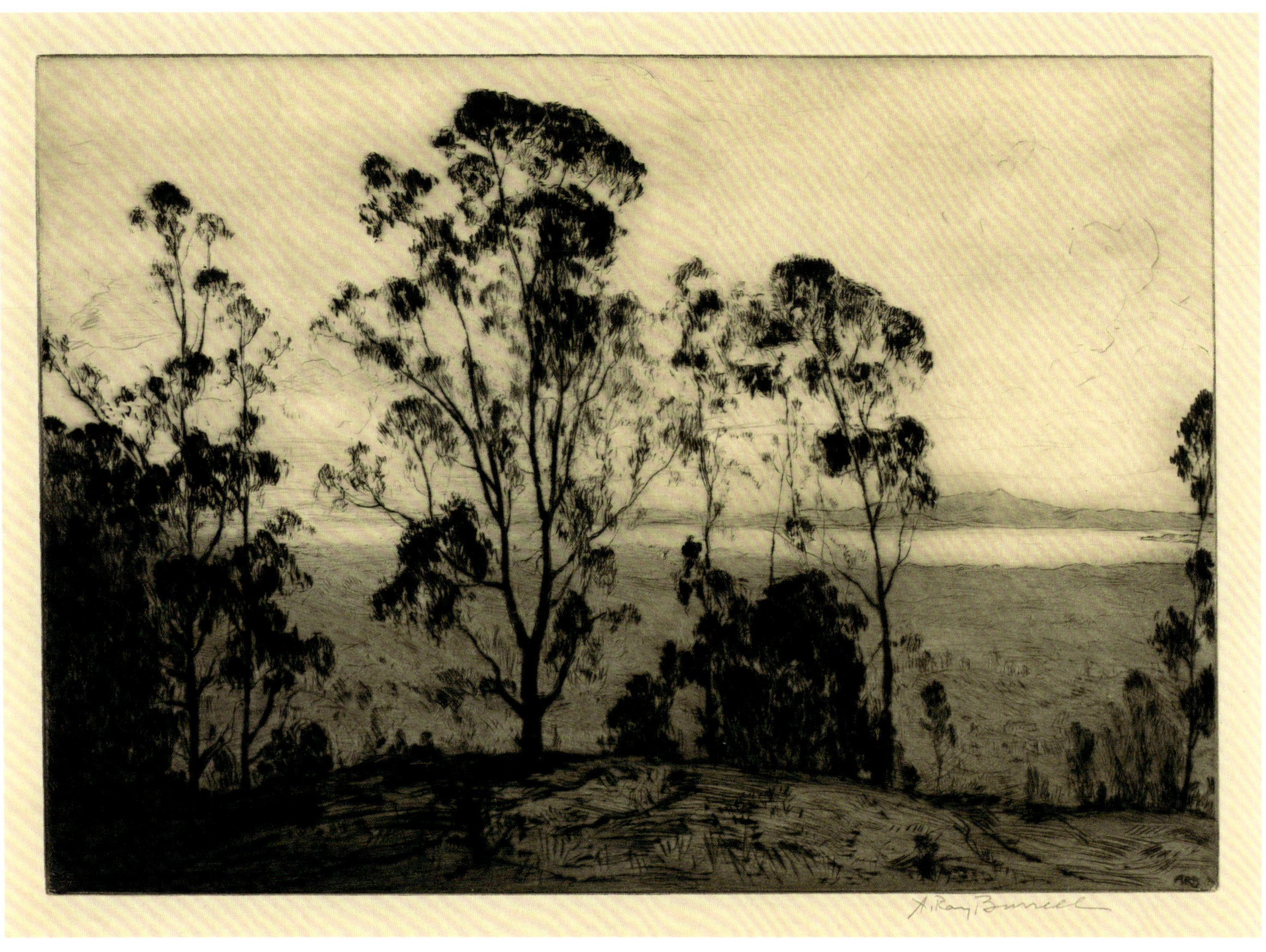

23. Alfred Ray Burrell (1877–1952), *Eucalyptus, Berkeley Hills,* 20th century

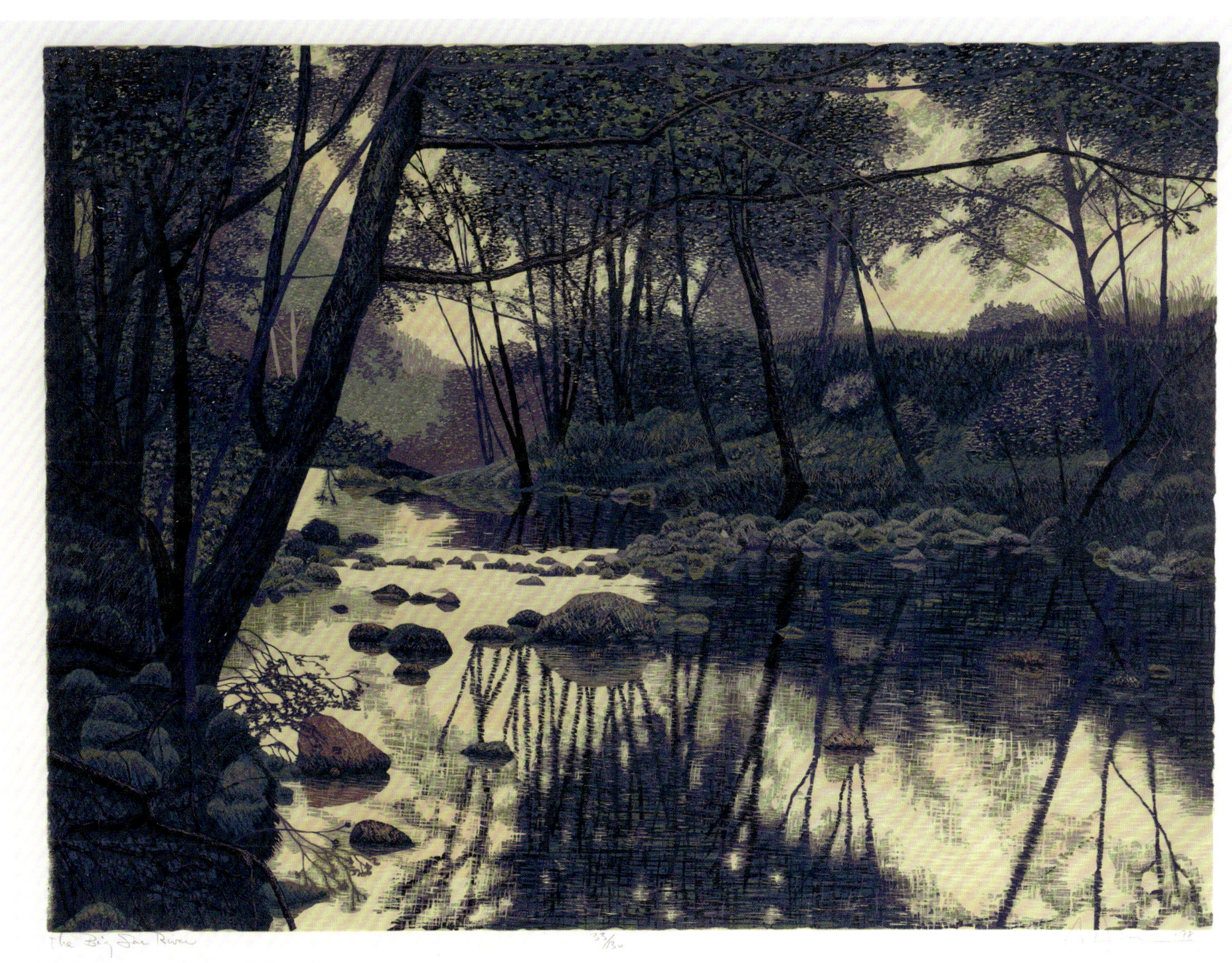

24. Gordon Mortensen (b. 1938), *The Big Sur River*, 1978

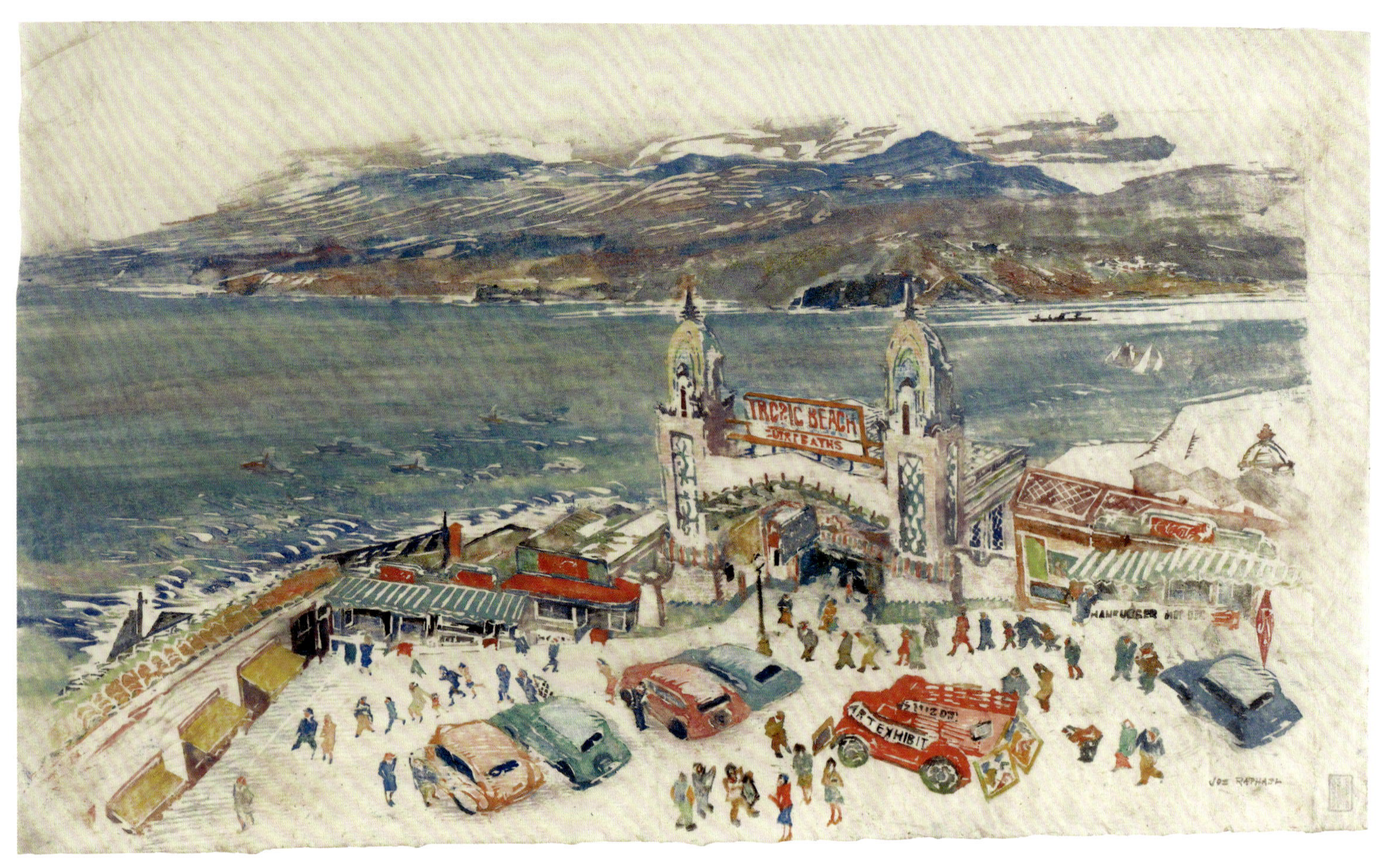

25. Joseph M. Raphael (1869–1950), *San Francisco Beach with Amusement Park, Opposite of Hills in Marin County*, 1939–1950

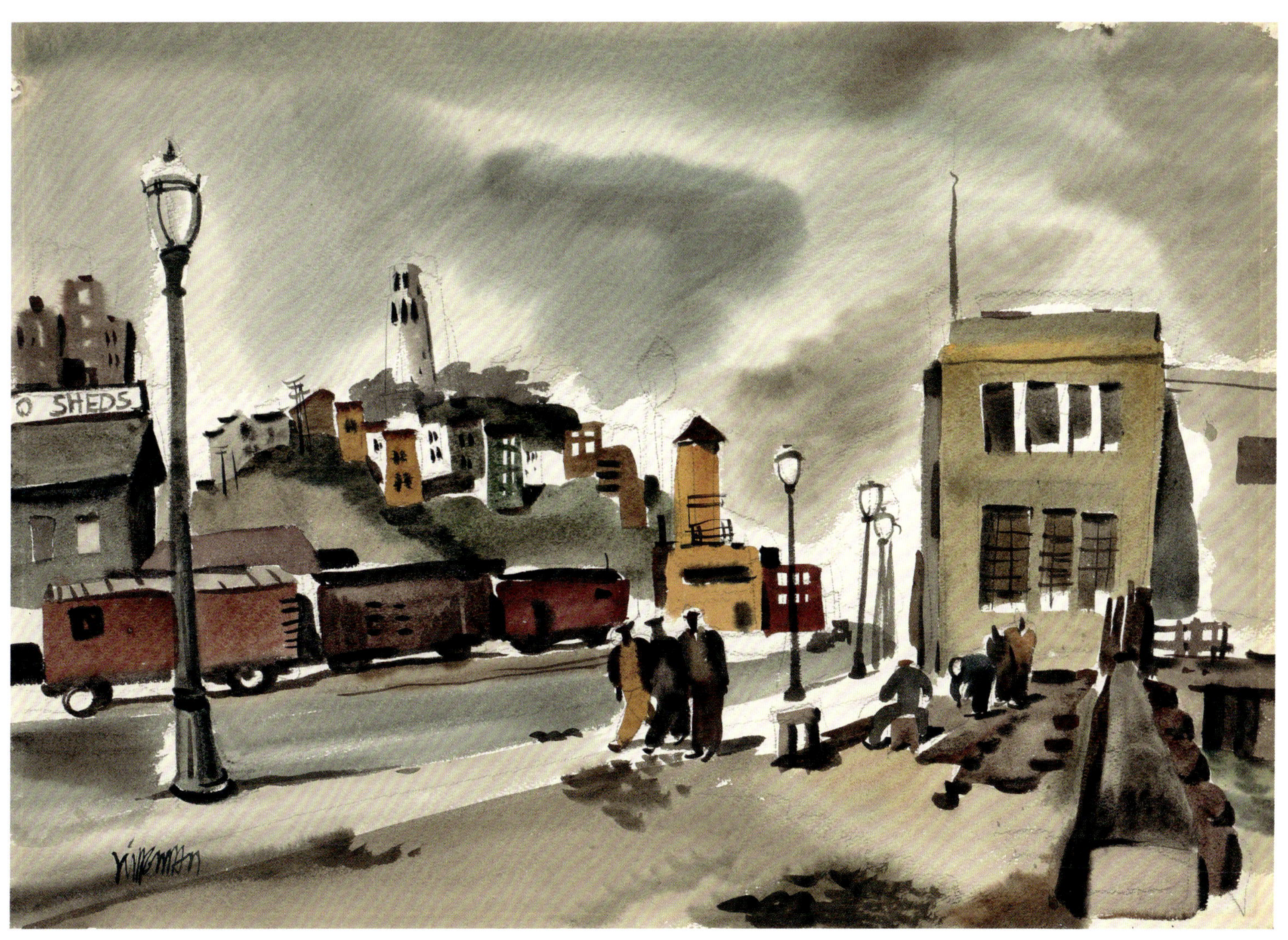

26. Dong Kingman (1911–2000), *Coit Tower and Embarcadero*, ca. 1935–1943

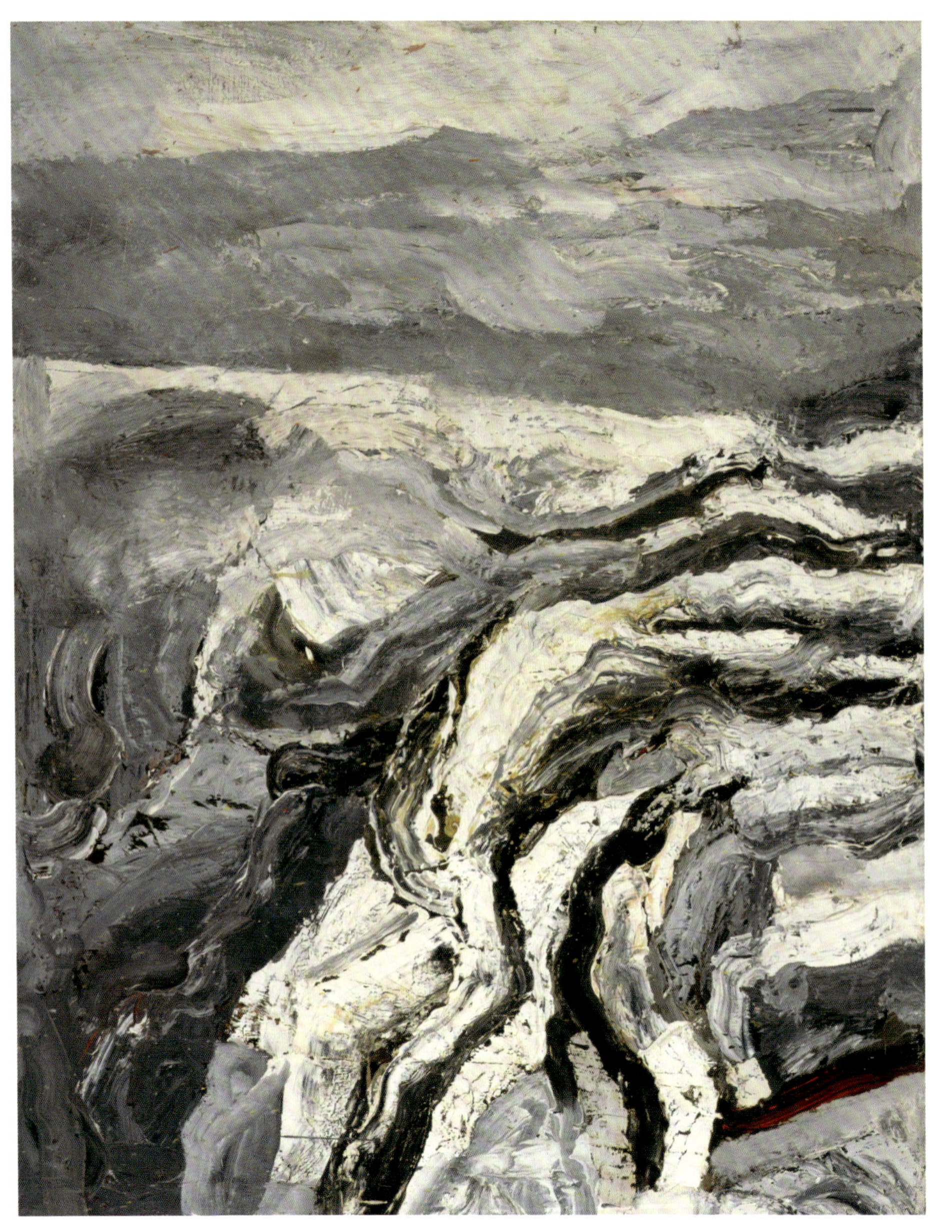

27. Jay DeFeo (1929–1989), *Mountain No. 2*, 1955

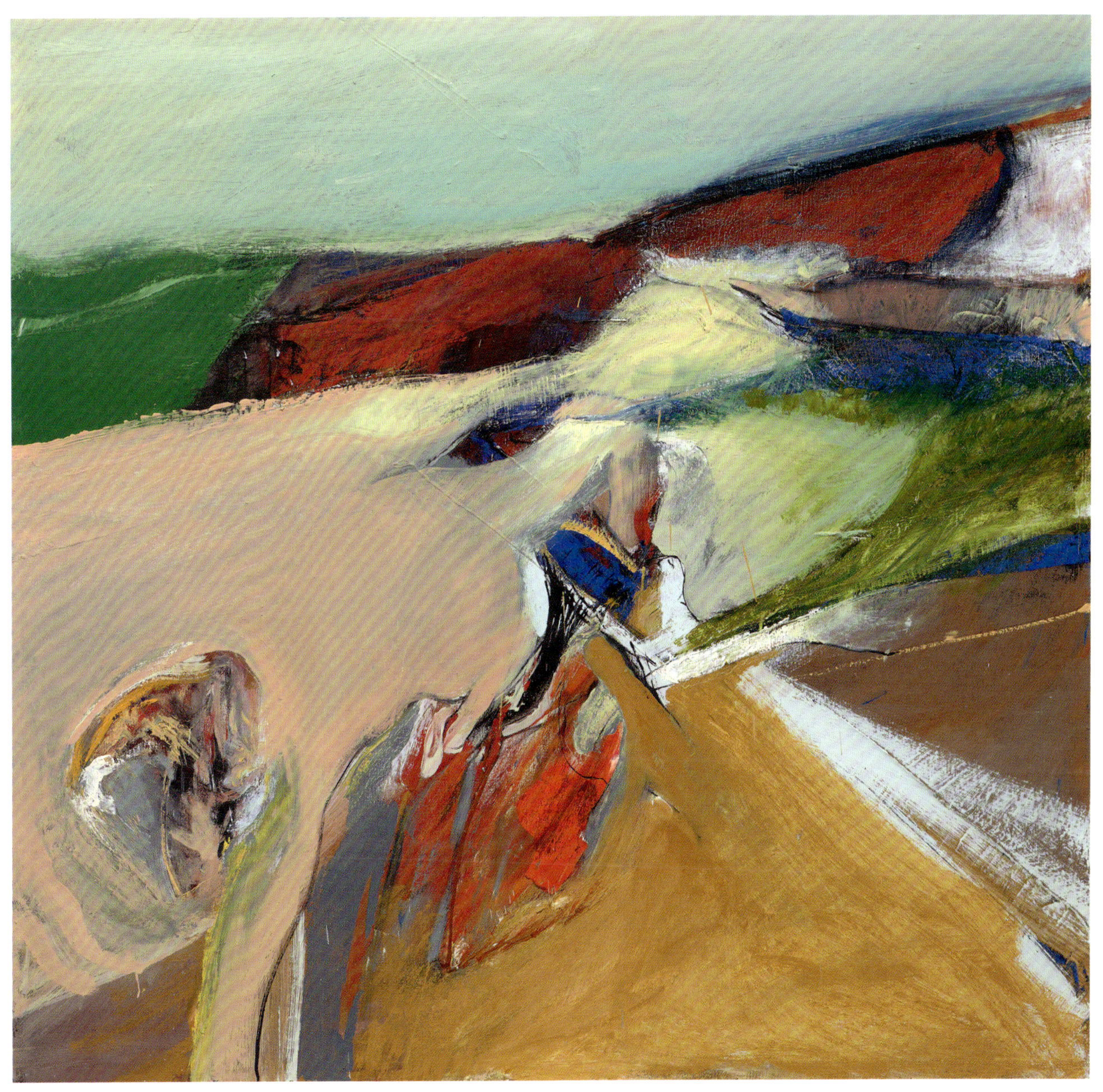

28. Bernice Bing (1936–1998), *Mayacamas No. 6, March 12, 1963*, 1963

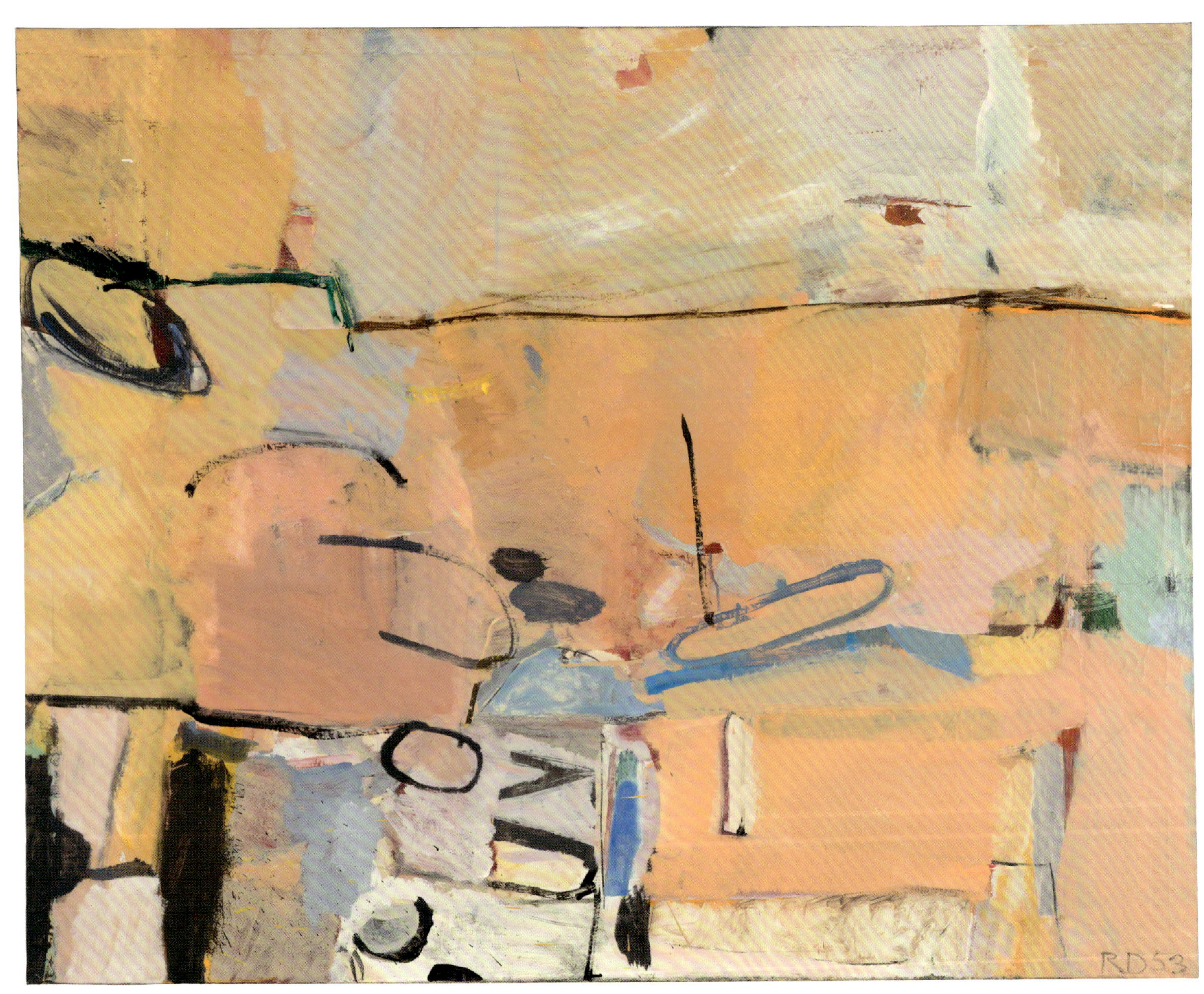

29. Richard Diebenkorn (1922–1993), *Berkeley #3*, 1953

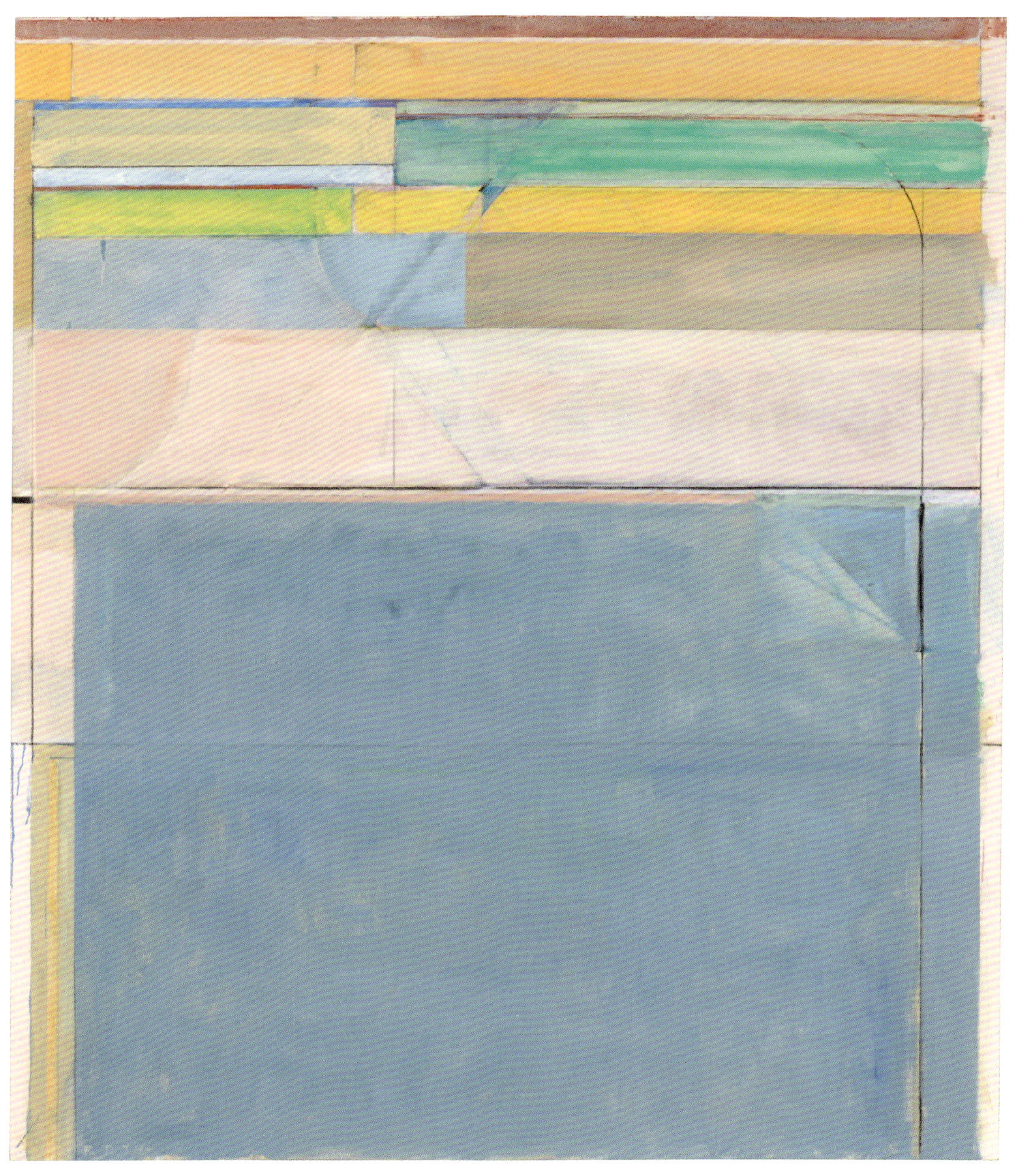

30. Richard Diebenkorn (1922–1993), *Ocean Park #116*, 1979

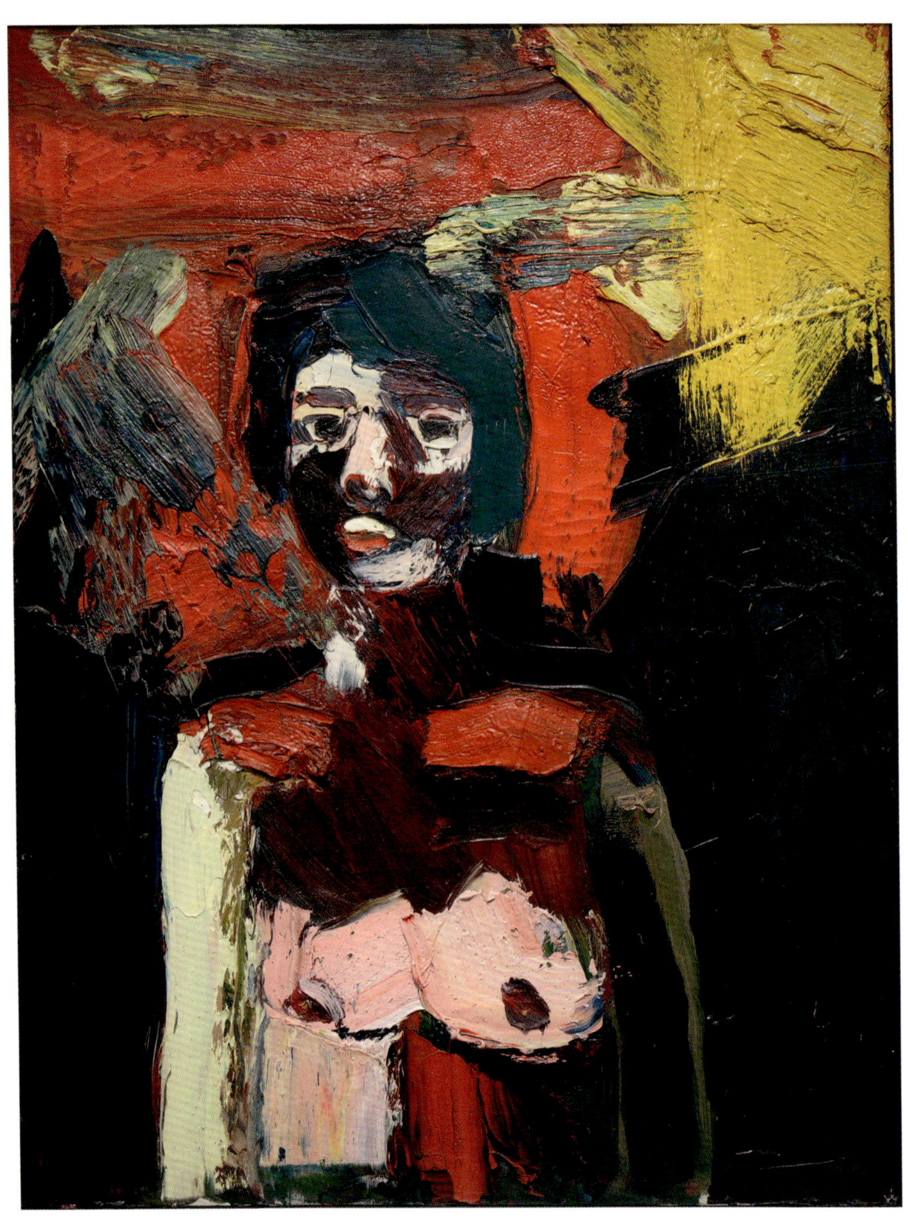

31. Joan Brown (1938–1990), *Young Girl*, 1962

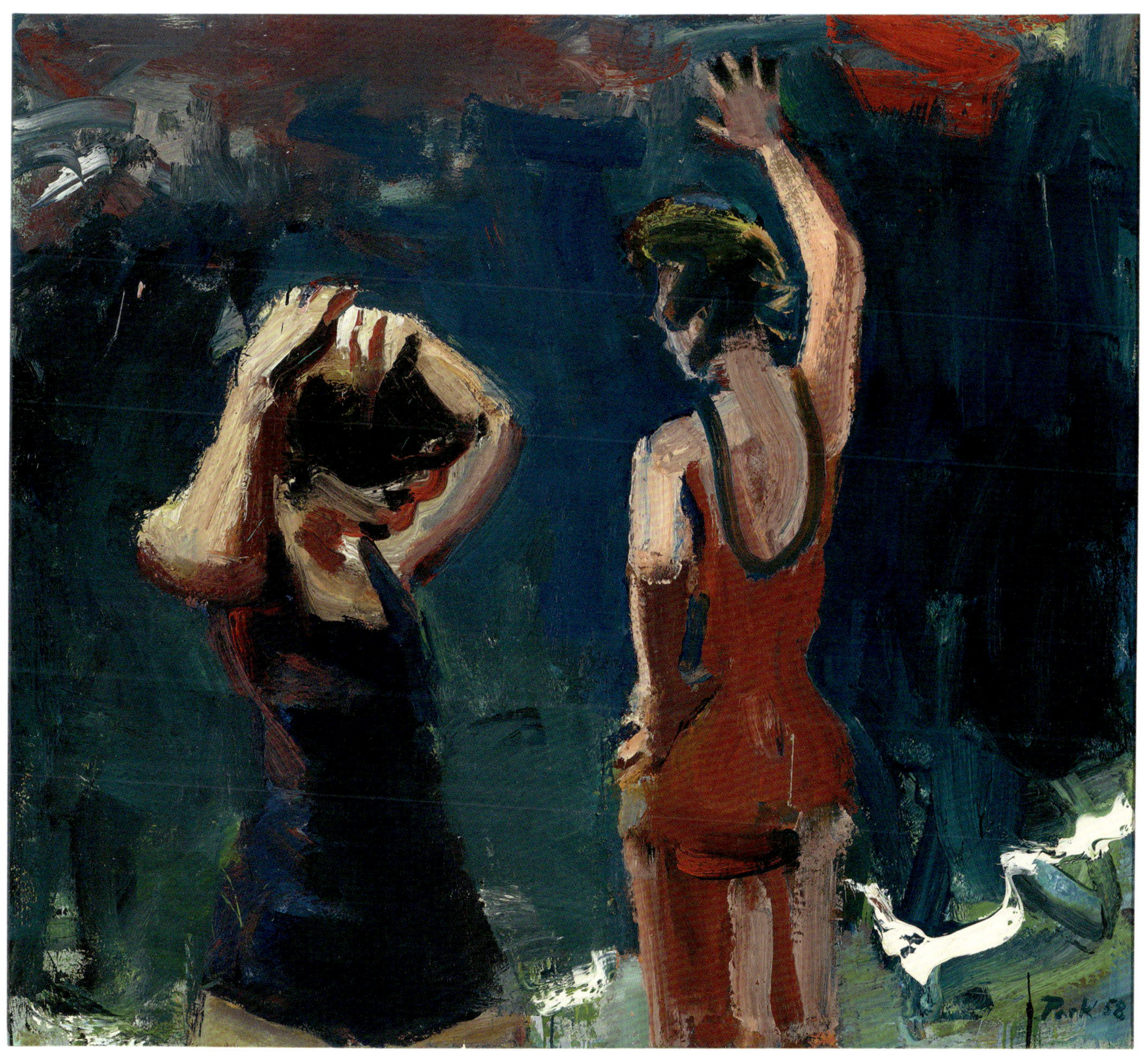

32. David Park (1911–1960), *Two Bathers*, 1958

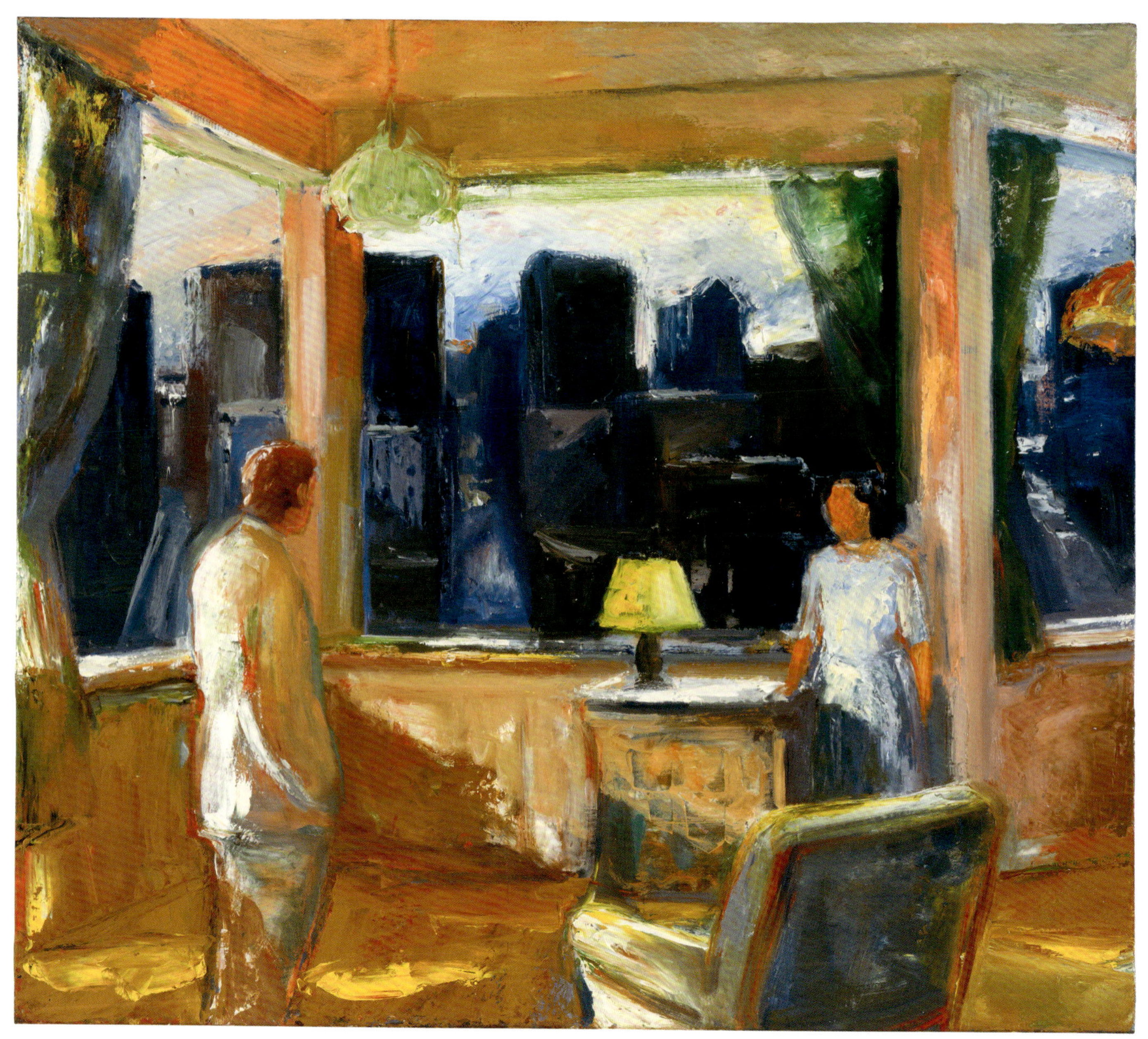

33. Elmer Bischoff (1916–1991), *Yellow Lampshade*, 1969

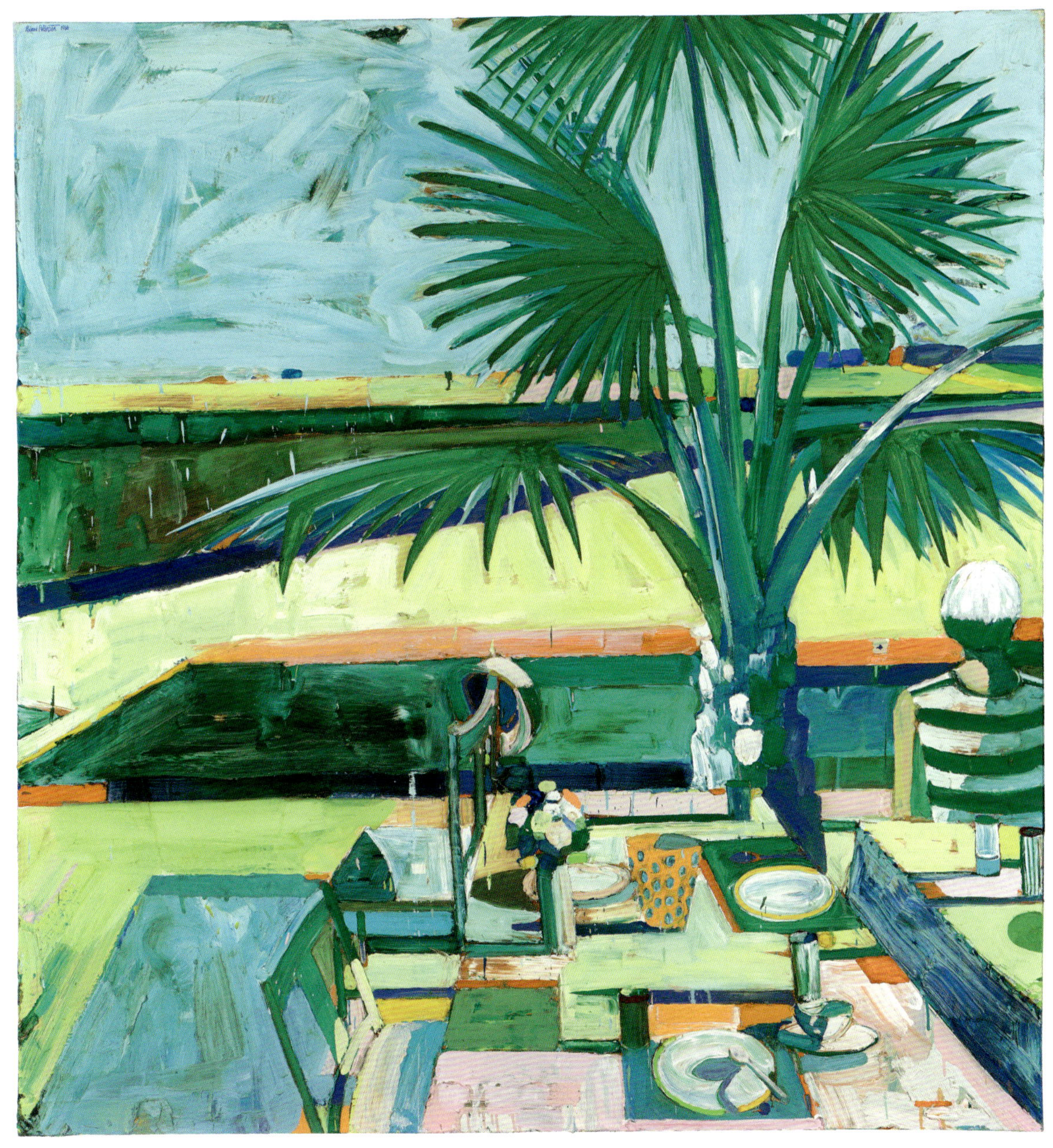

34. Roland Petersen (b. 1926), *Palm Sunday*, 1966

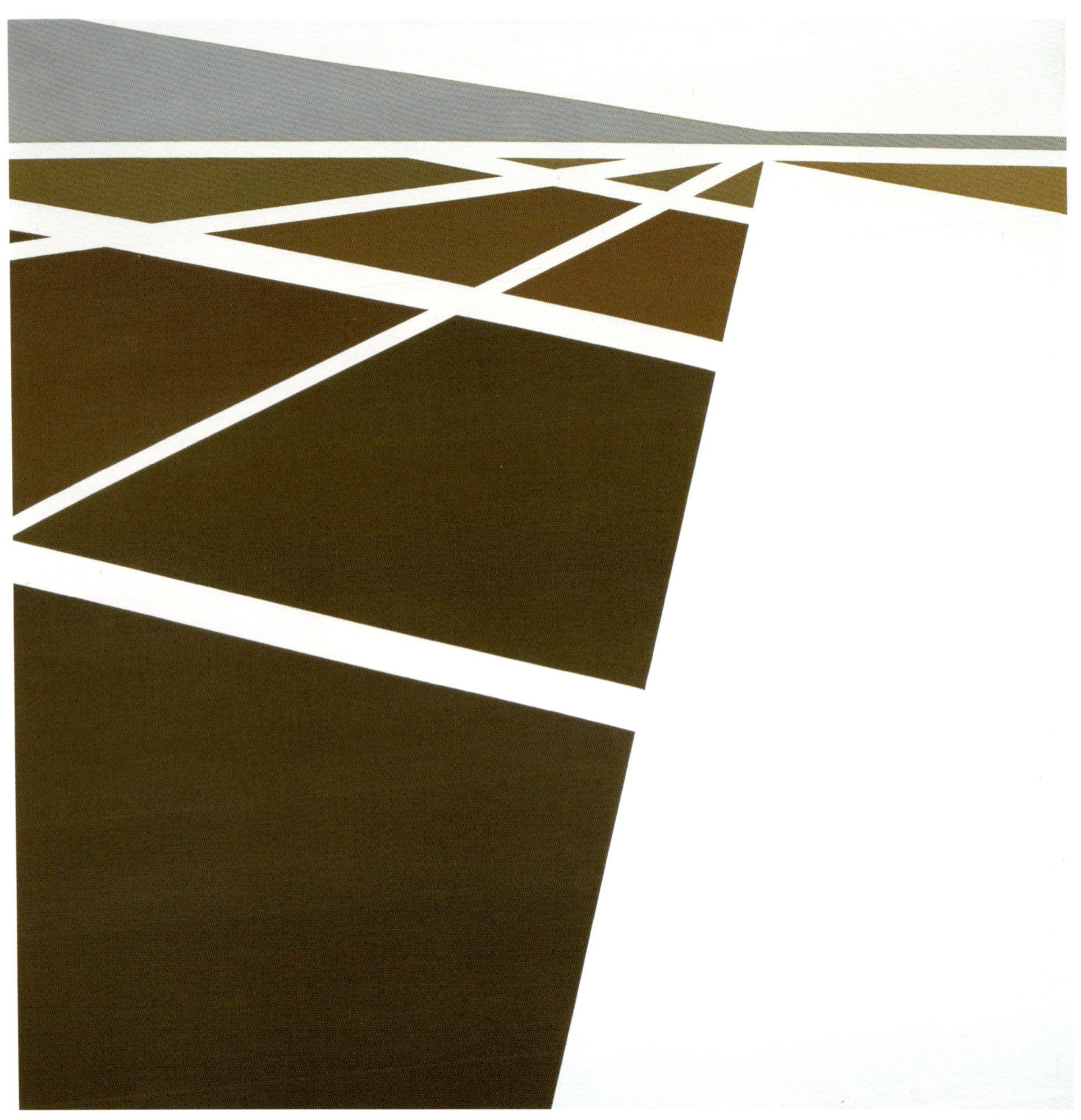

35. Helen Lundeberg (1908–1999), *Waterways III*, 1962

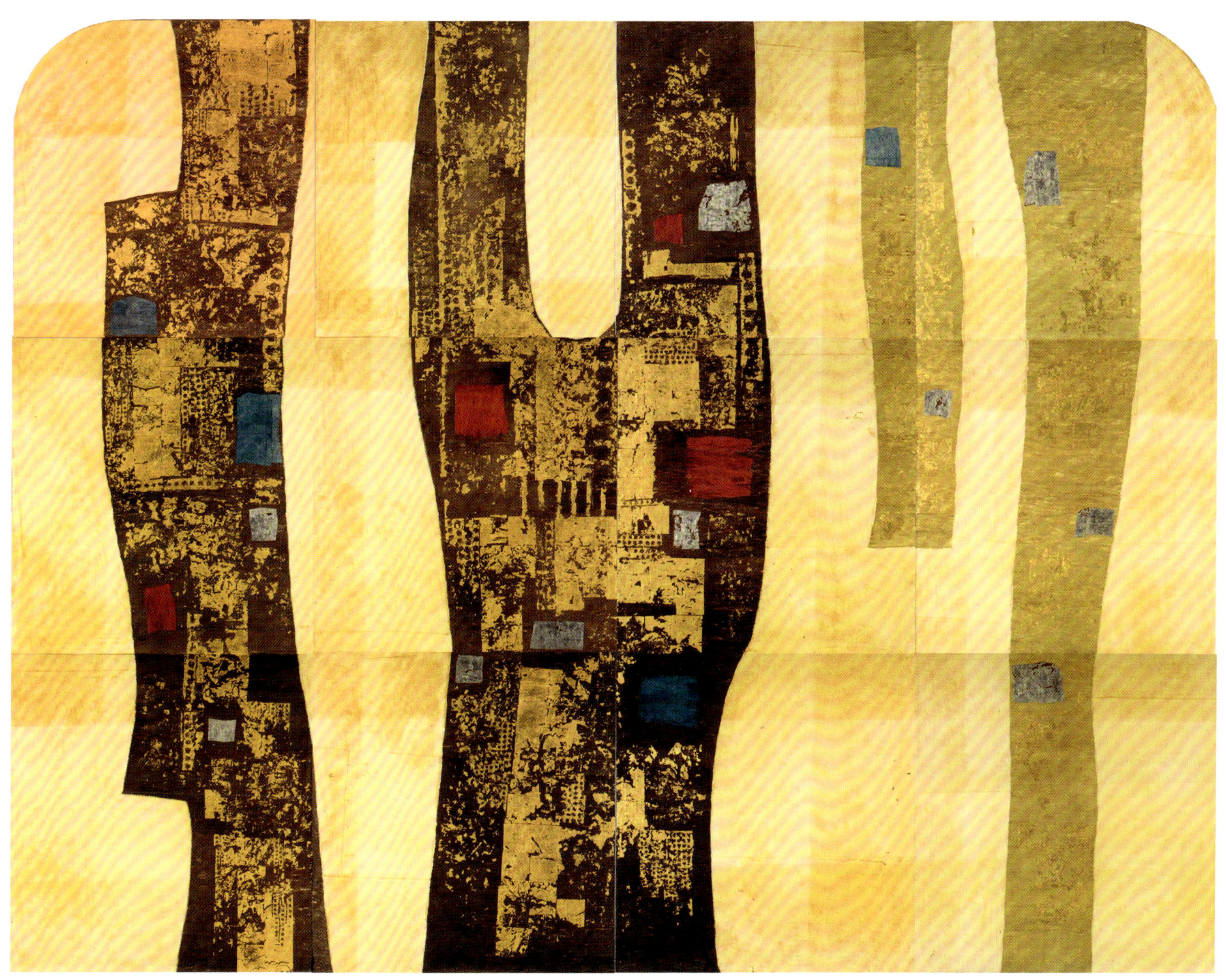

36. Yu-ho Tseng (1924–2017), *Mural #2,* from *Western Frontier*, 1964

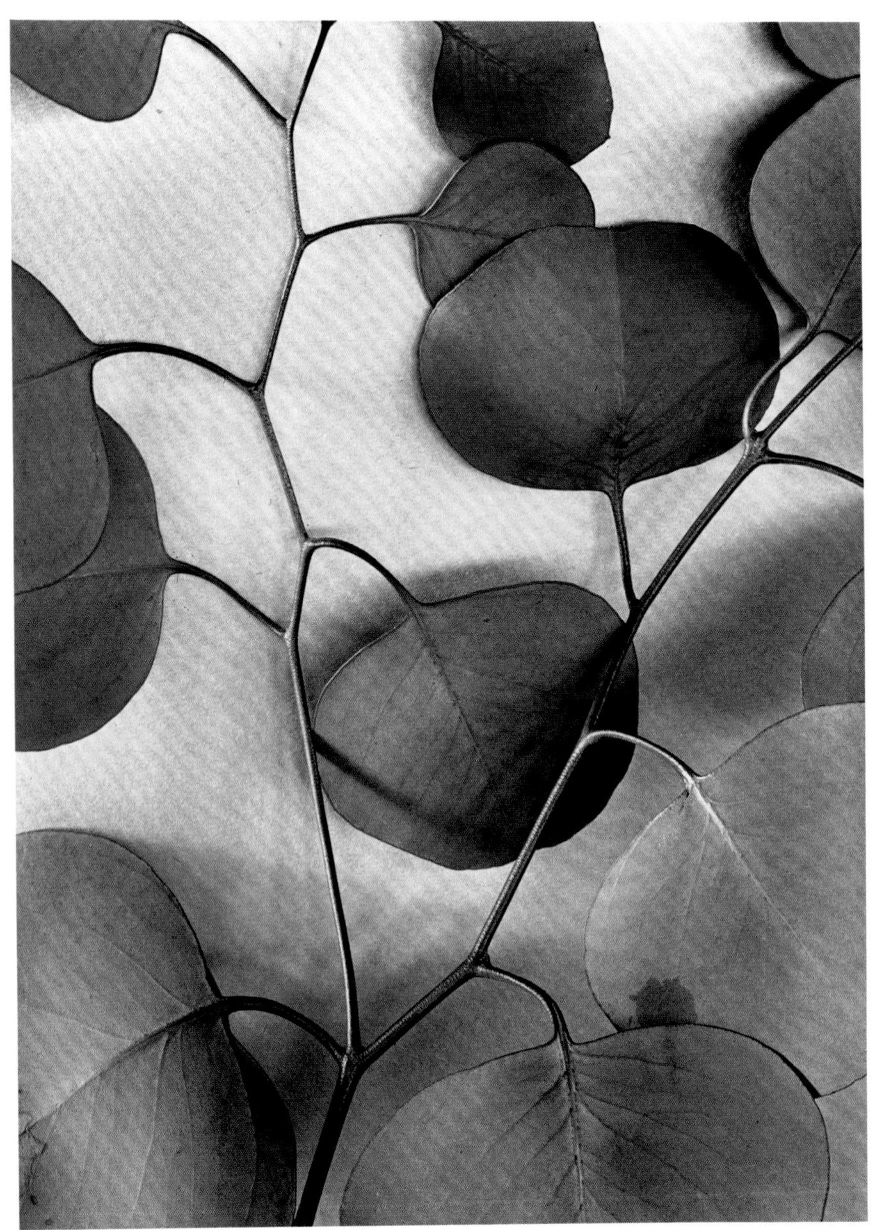

37. Alma Lavenson (1897–1989), *Eucalyptus Leaves,* 1933, printed 1987

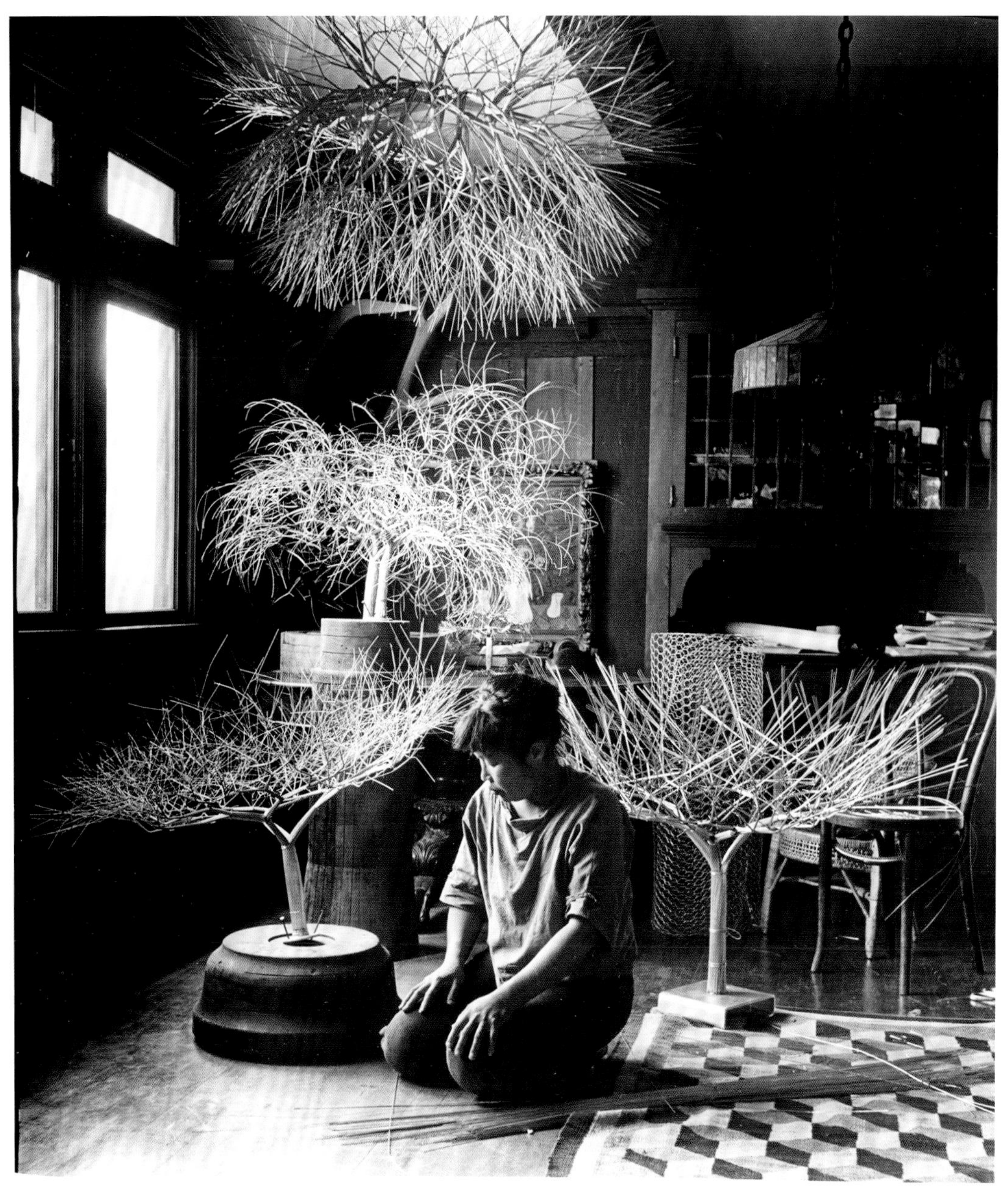

38. Imogen Cunningham (1883–1976), Untitled (Ruth Asawa kneeling on floor of dining room with tied wire sculpture), 1963

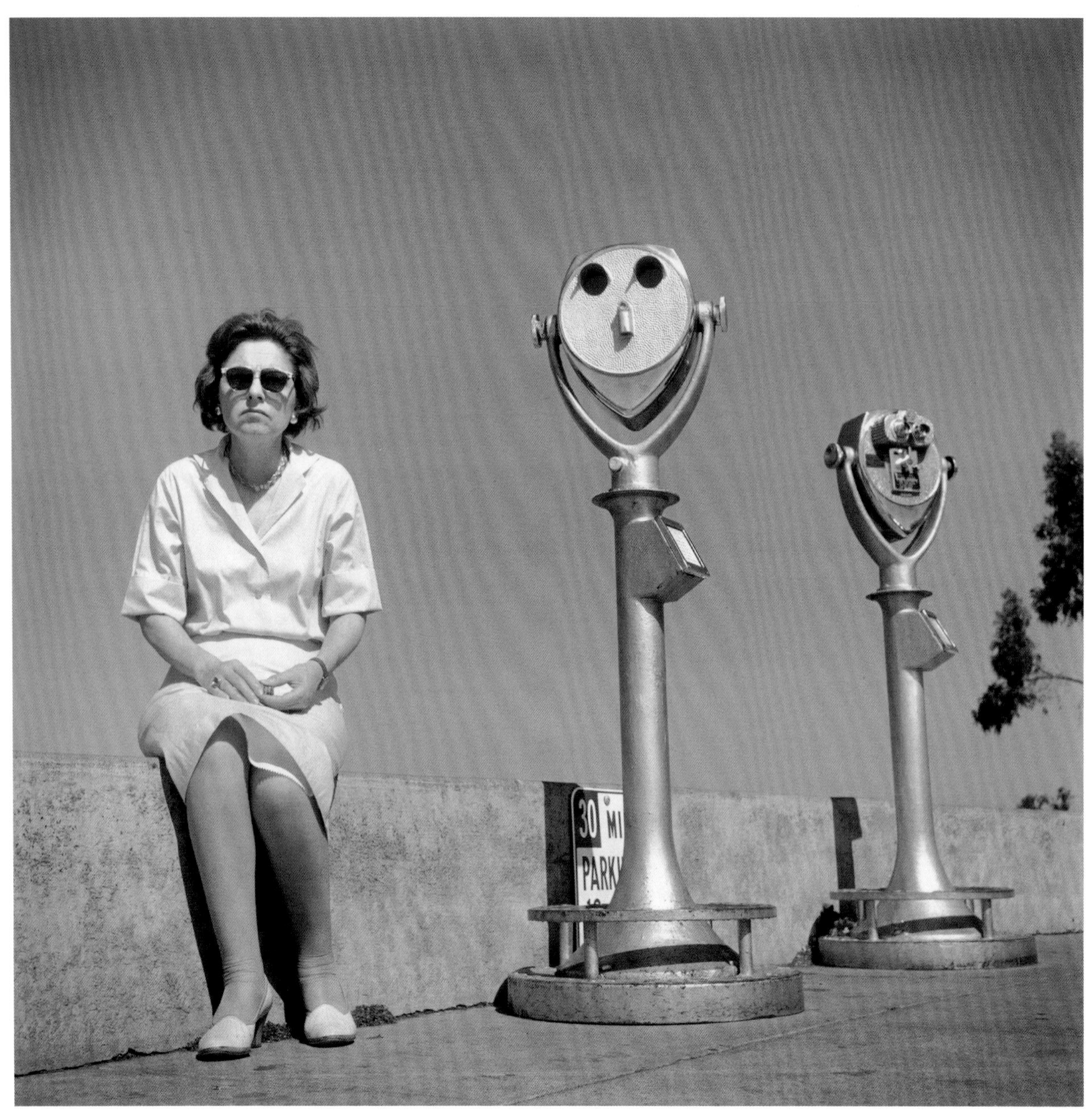

39. Arthur Tress (b. 1940), *Untitled (Coit Tower)*, from the series *San Francisco*, 1964, printed 2010–2011

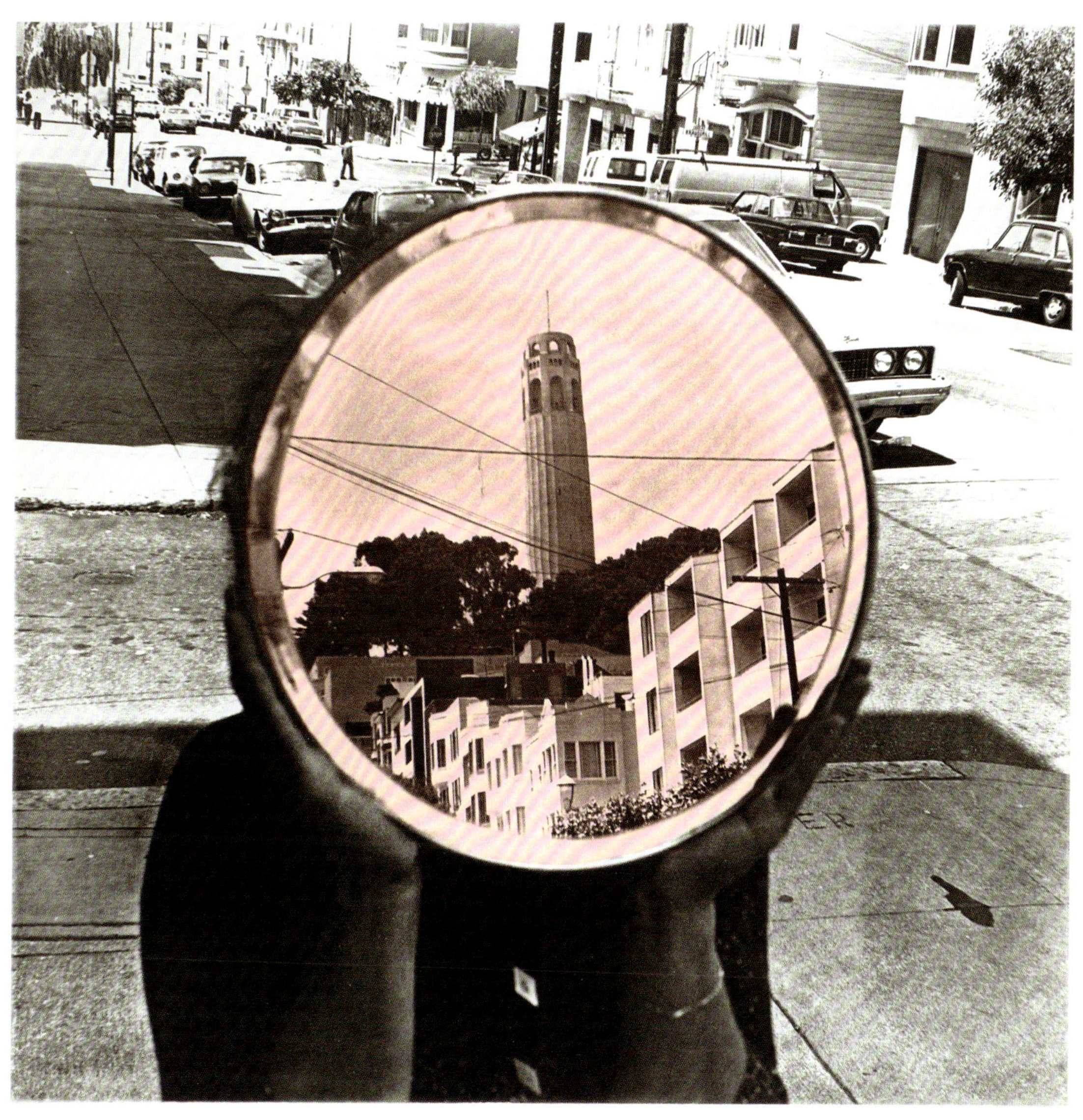

40. Iain Baxter (now Iain Baxter&, b. 1936), *Coit Tower*, from the set *Reflected San Francisco Beauty Spots*, 1979

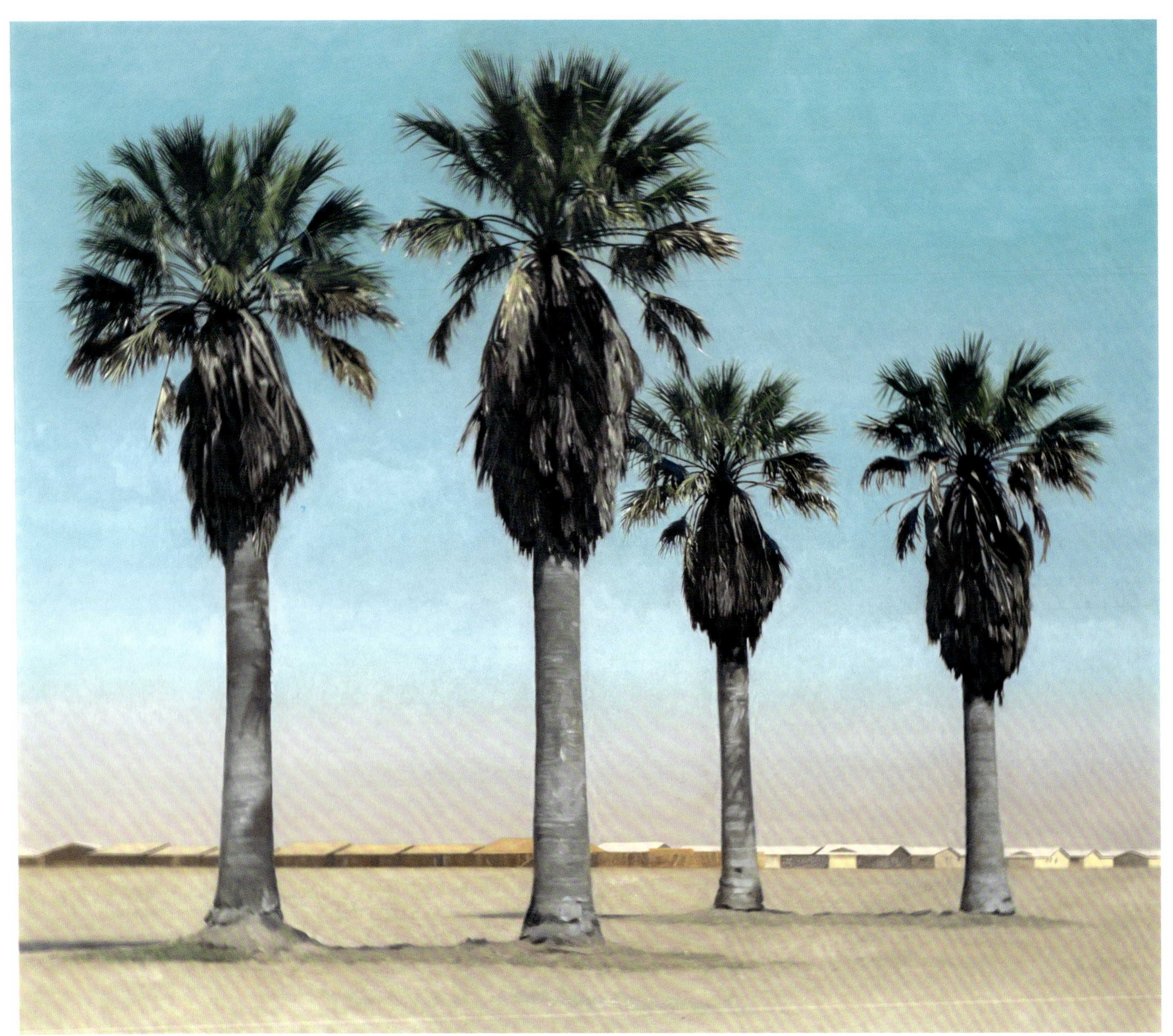

41. Robert Bechtle (b. 1932), *Four Palm Trees*, 1969

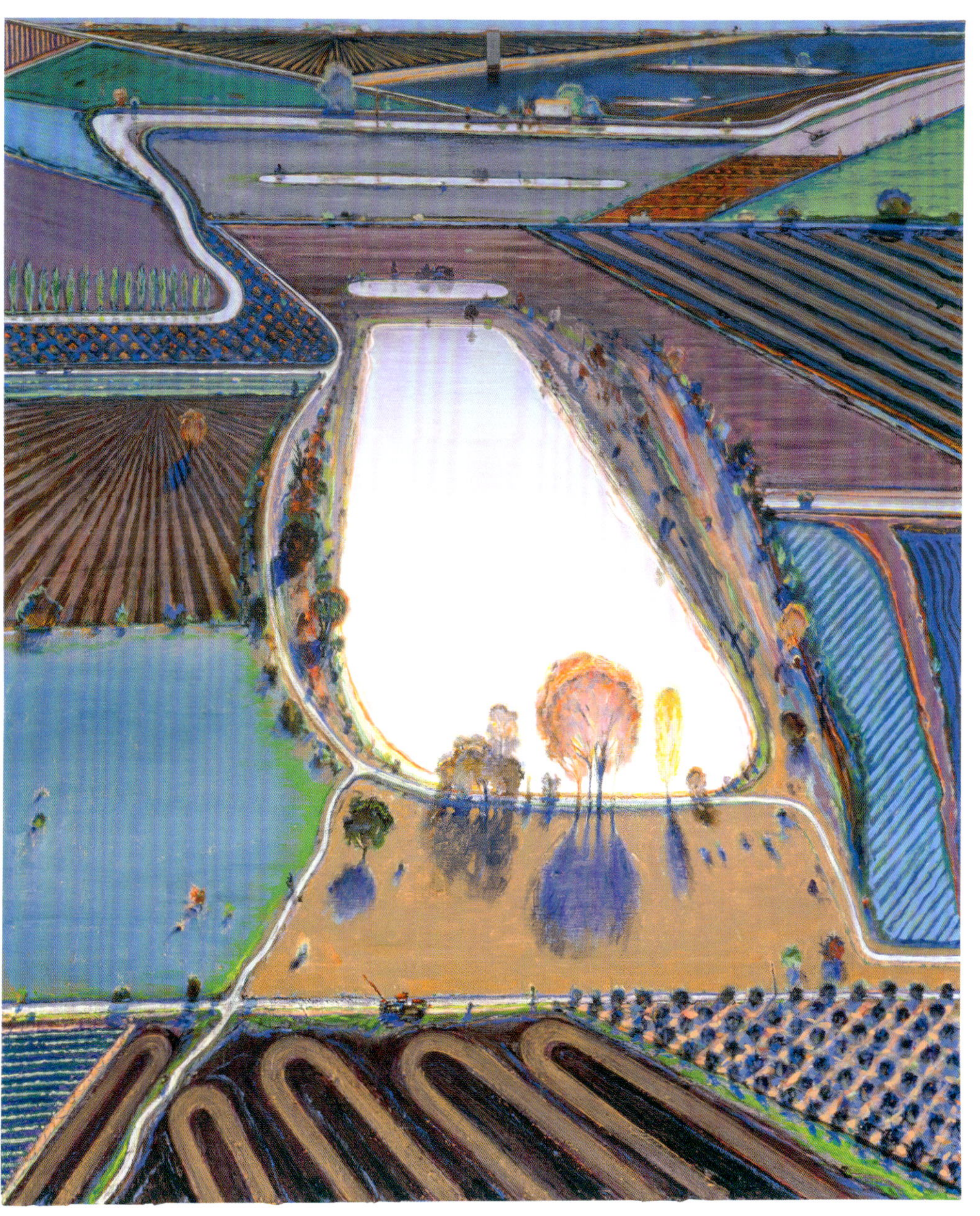

42. Wayne Thiebaud (1920–2021), *Ponds and Streams*, 2001

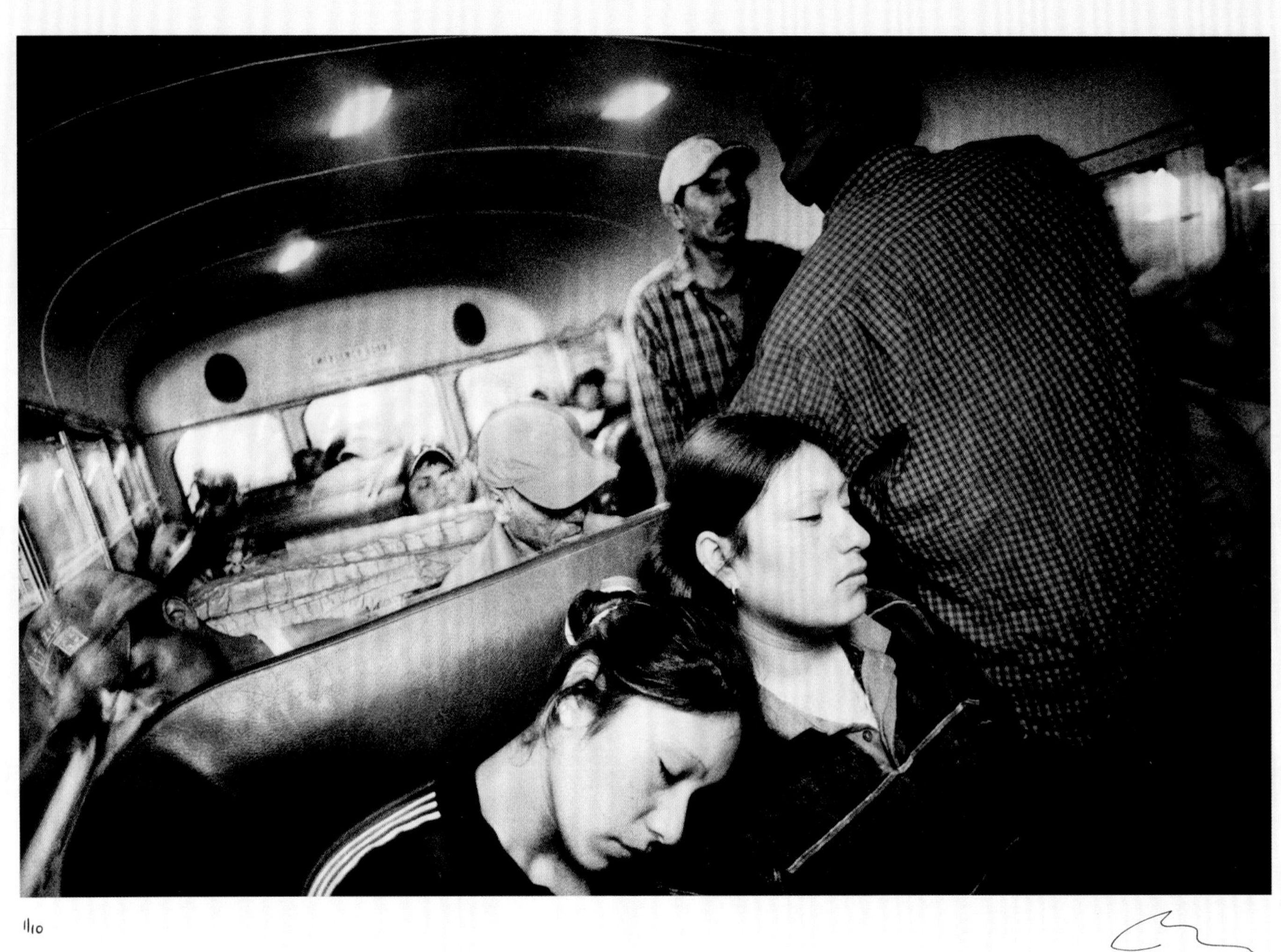

43. Matt Black (b. 1970), *Riding to Work in a Farm Labor Bus, Fresno, California*, 2004, printed 2016

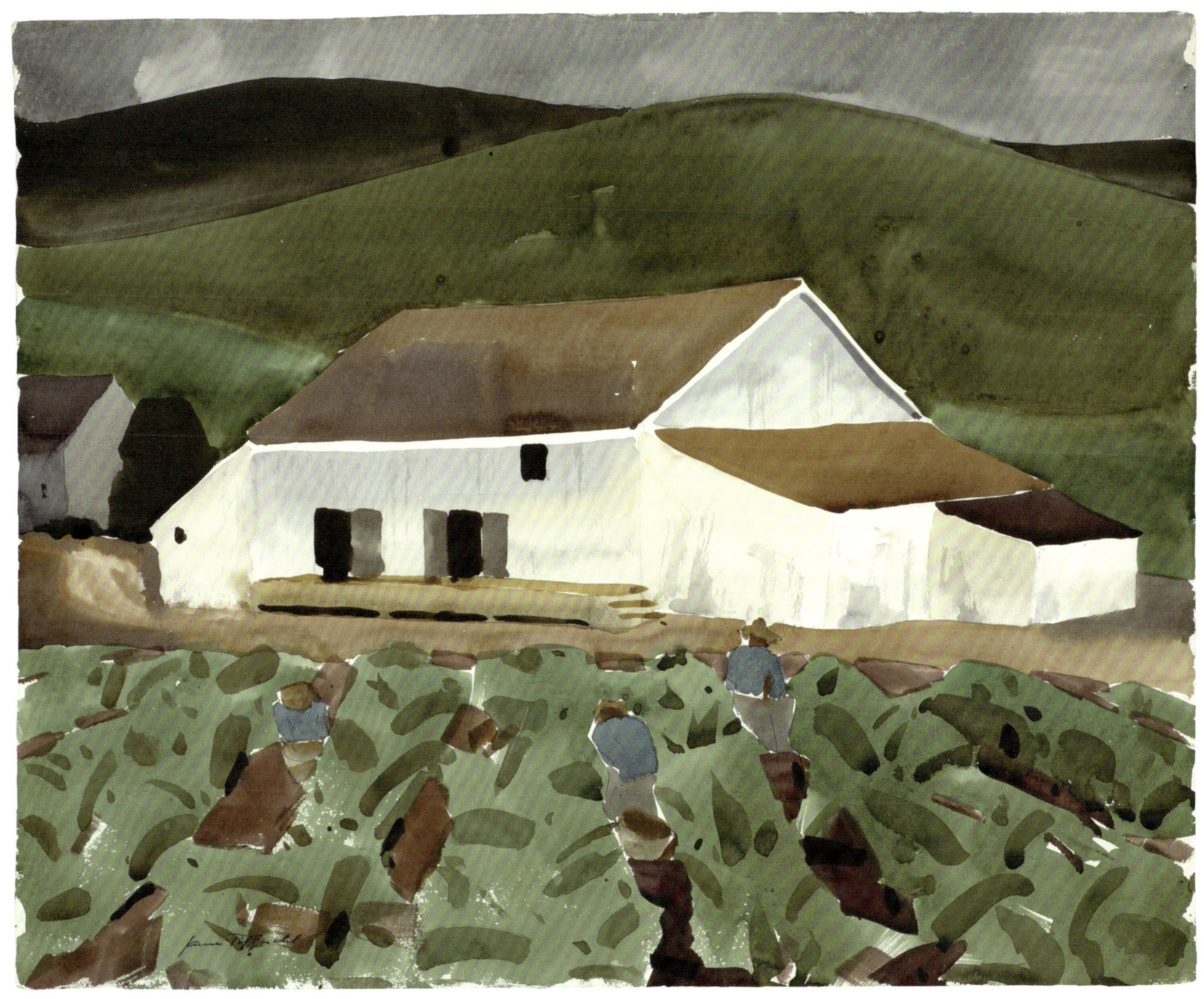

44. James Edward Fitzgerald (1899–1971), *Artichoke Ranch*, 1939

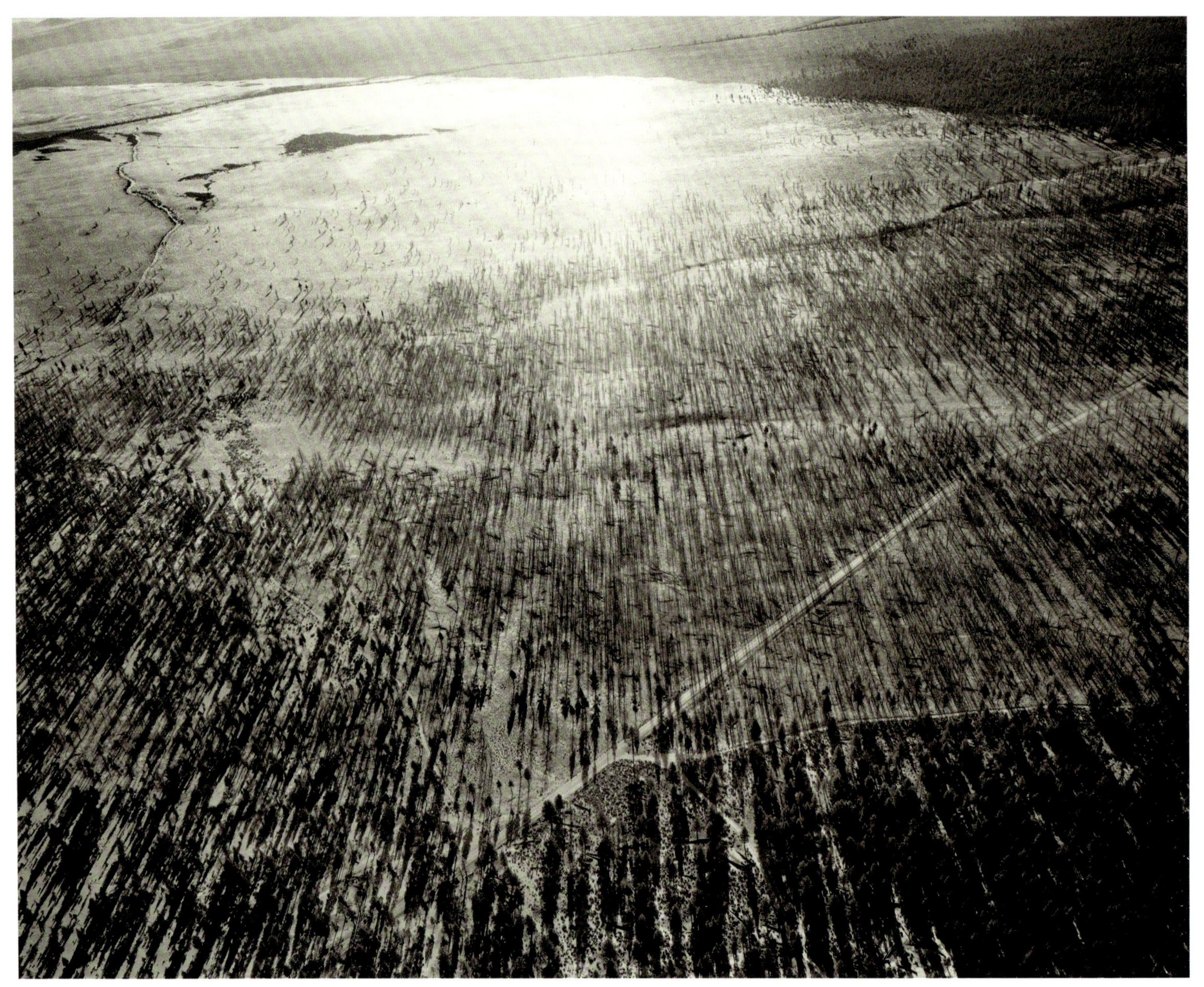

45. Michael Light (b. 1963), *Mono Craters 07.17.06 #10: Burned Jeffrey Pine Forest and Tephra Flow Looking Southeast, Highway 120 at Right, Mono Basin, California*, 2006

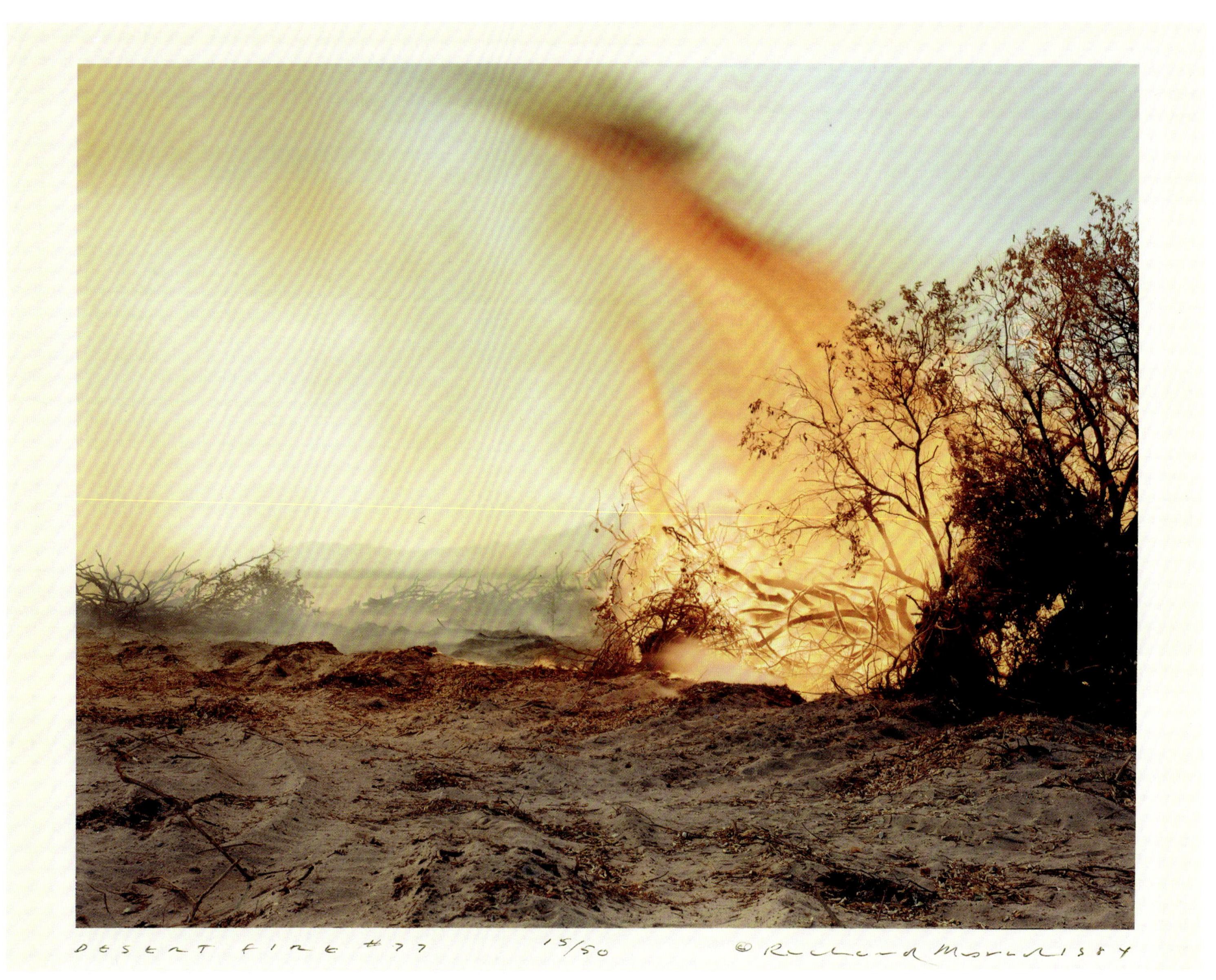

46. Richard Misrach (b. 1949), *Desert Fire #77*, 1984

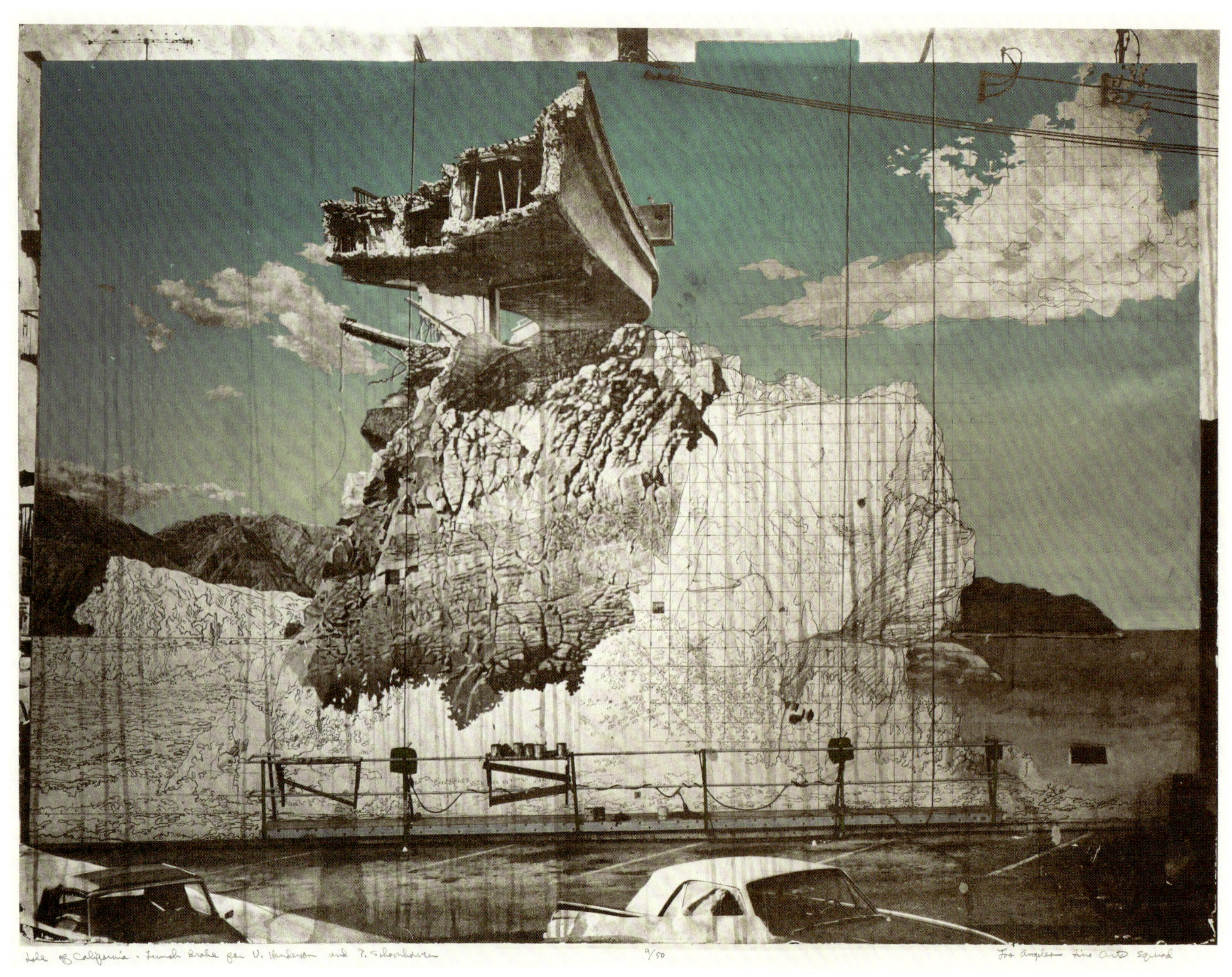

47. L.A. Fine Arts Squad (1969–1972), Victor Henderson (b. 1939), and Terry Schoonhoven (1945–2001), *Isle of California: Lunch Brake for V. Henderson and T. Schoonhoven*, 1973

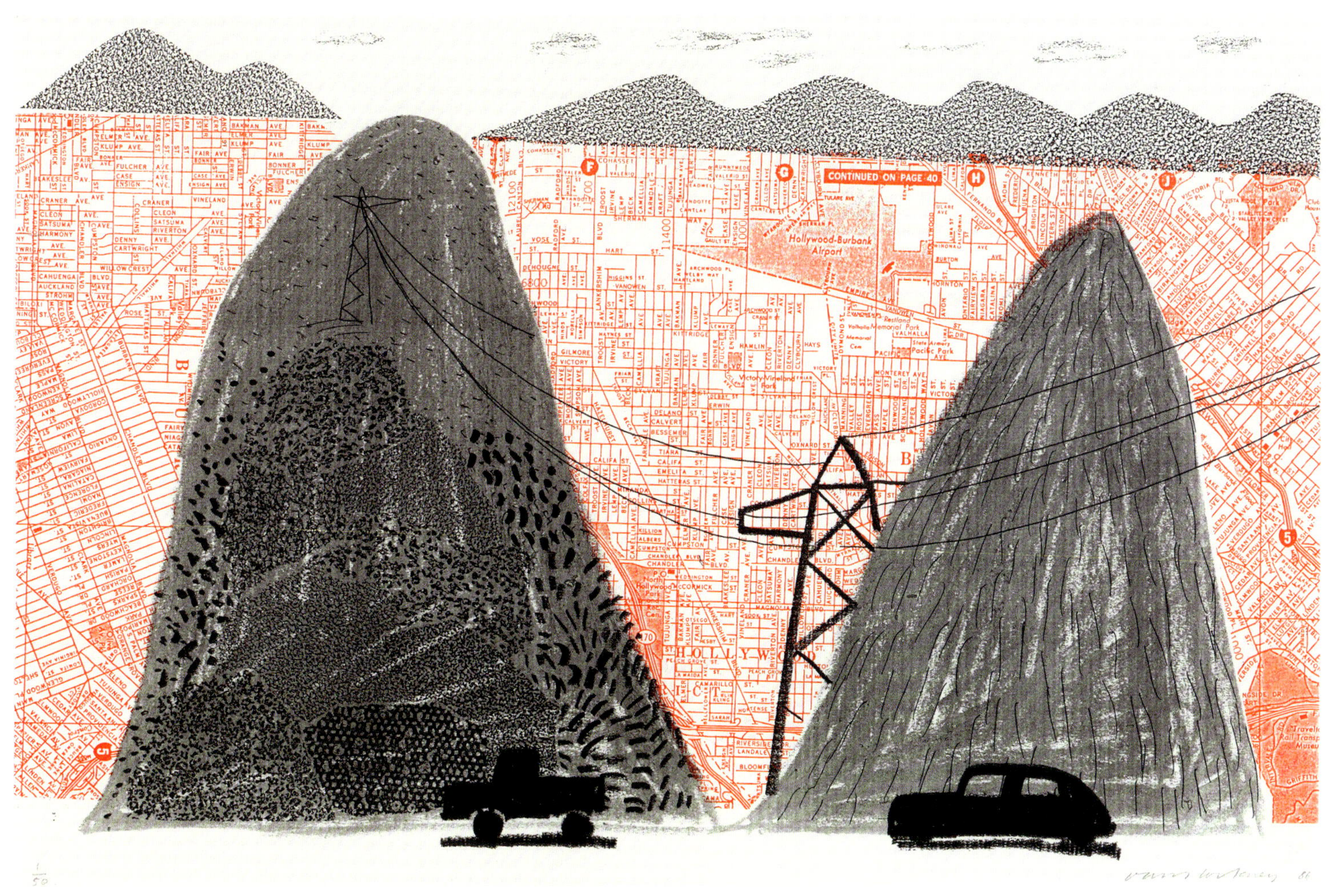

48. David Hockney (b. 1937), *Mulholland Drive, June 1986*, 1986

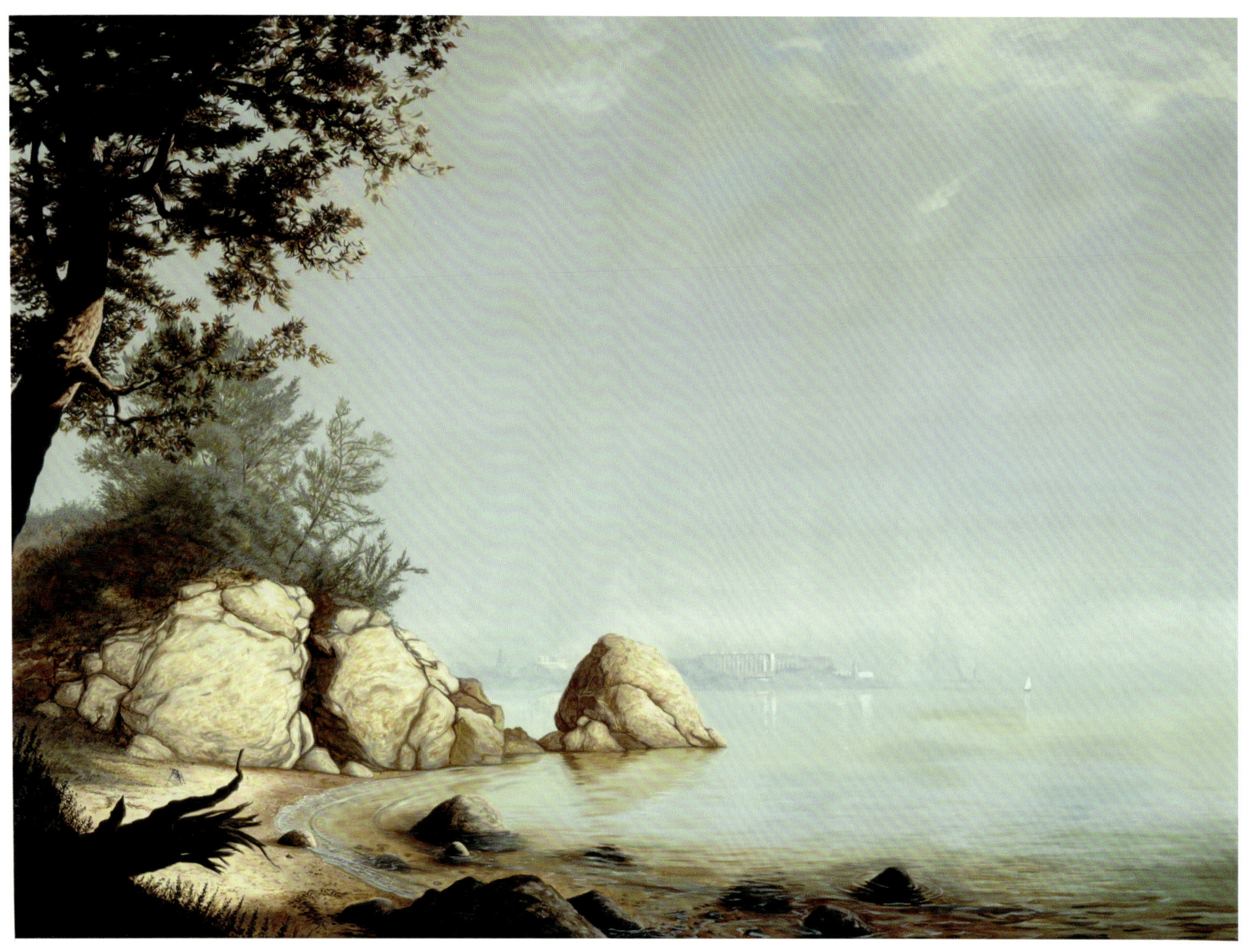

49. Sandow Birk (b. 1962), *Fog over San Quentin State Prison, San Quentin, California*, from the series *Prisonation*, 2001

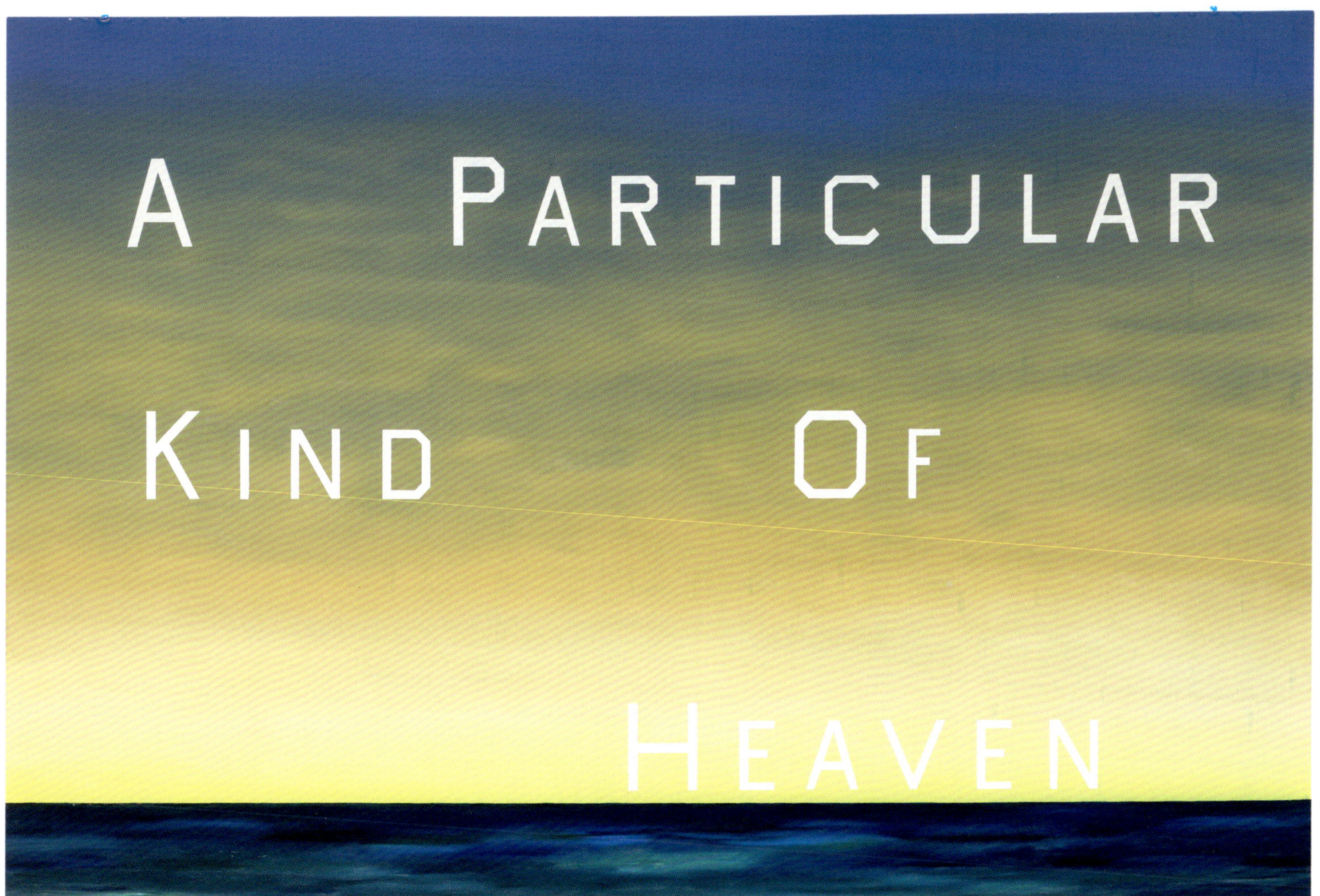

50. Ed Ruscha (b. 1937), *A Particular Kind of Heaven* (middle panel), 1983/2005

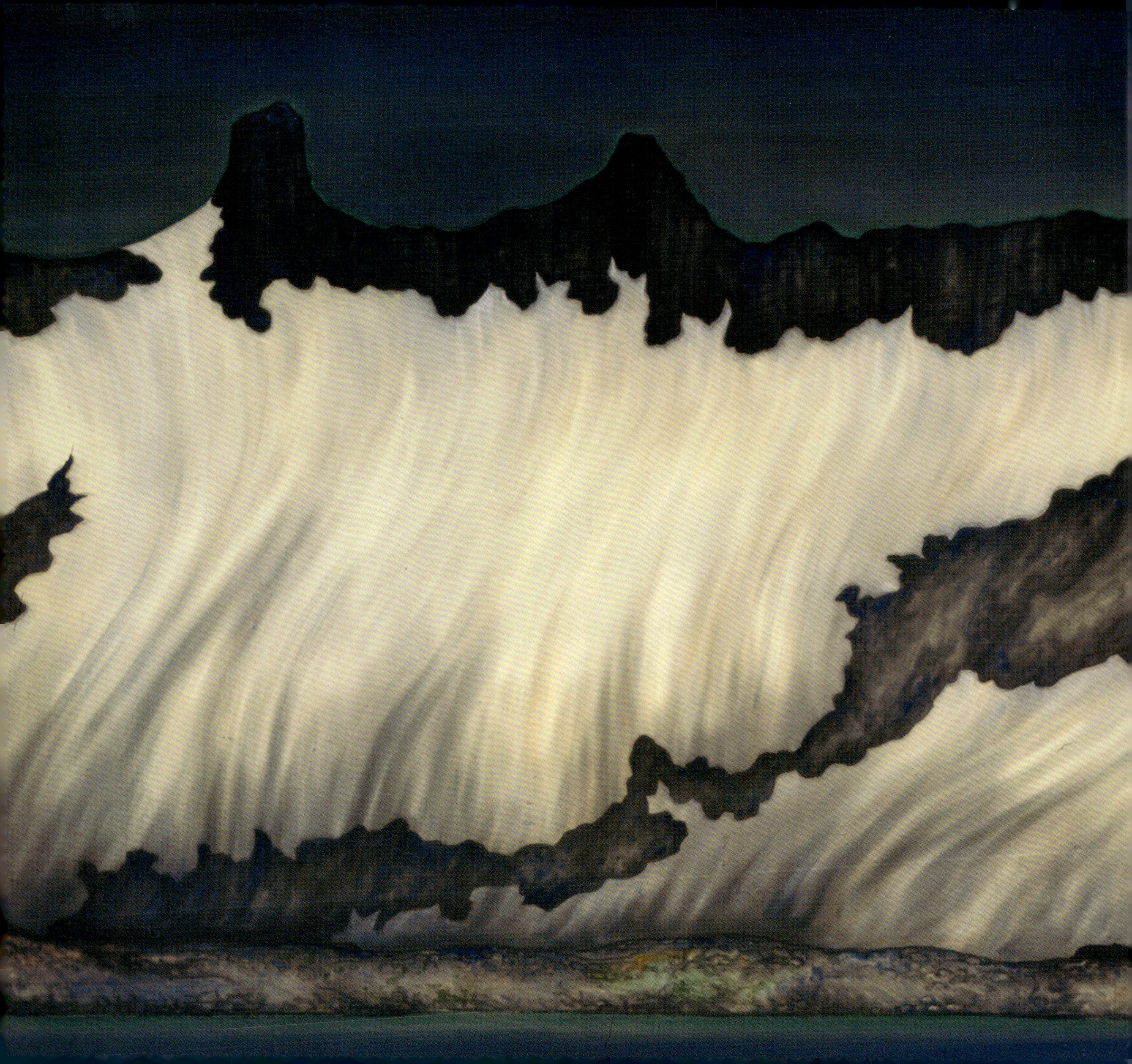

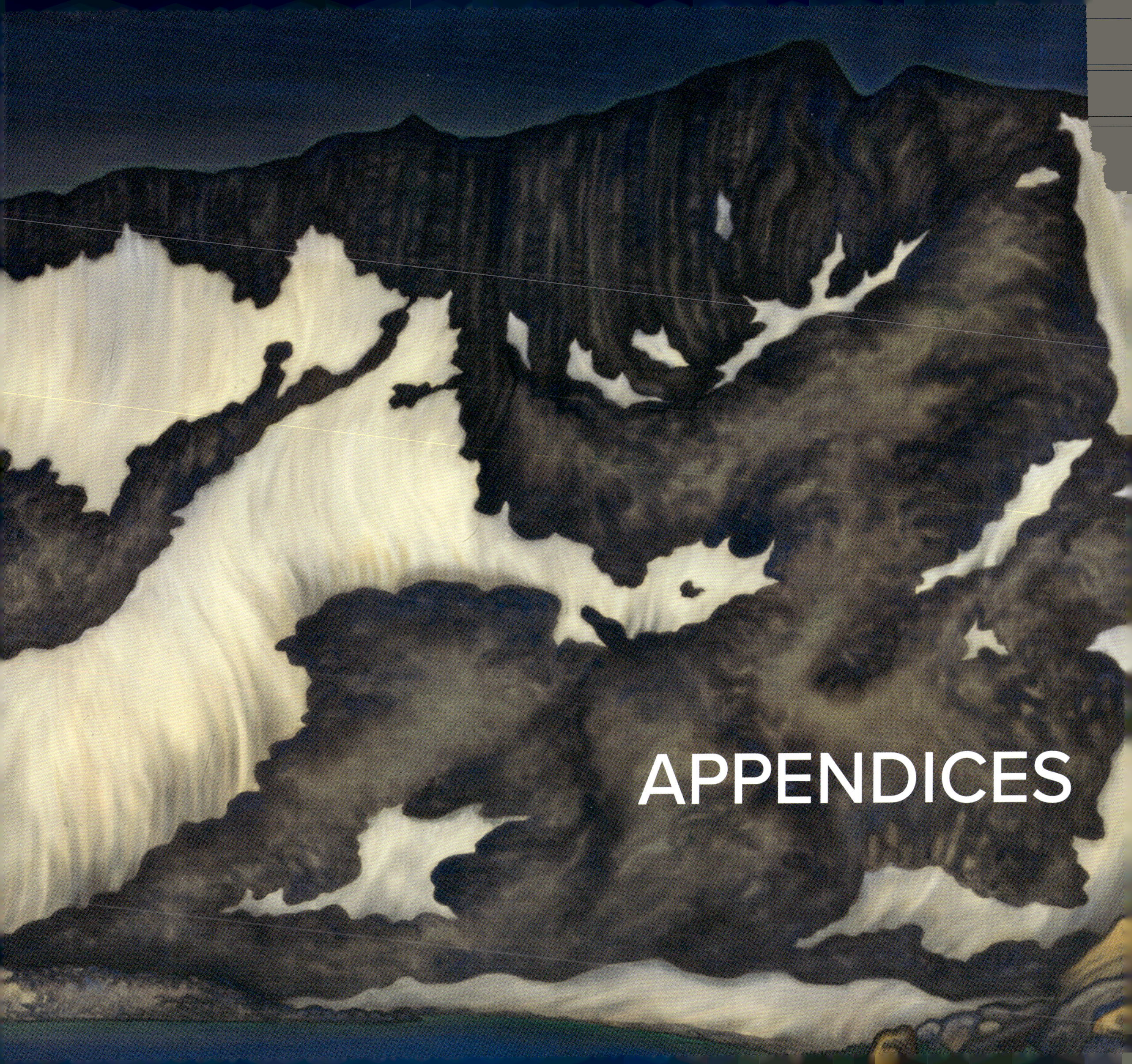

APPENDICES

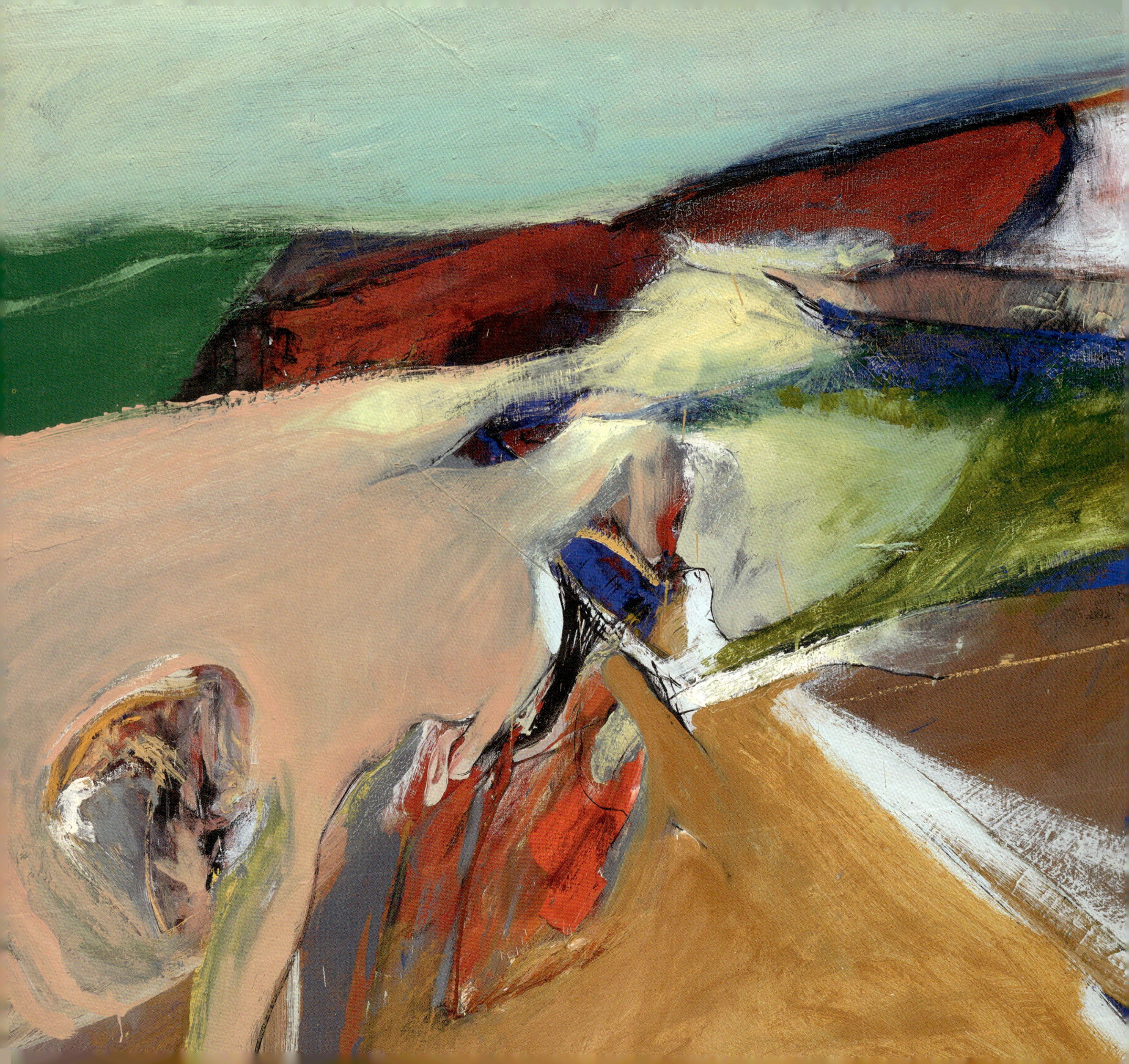

LIST OF ILLUSTRATIONS

IAIN BAXTER (now IAIN BAXTER&, b. 1936)
Nancy Anello (b. 1951), printer
Crown Point Press (active 20th century), publisher
Coit Tower, from the set *Reflected San Francisco Beauty Spots*, 1979
Photoetching with aquatint printed in pink, 23 5/8 x 23 7/8 in. (60.2 x 60.8 cm)
Crown Point Press Archive, gift of Kathan Brown
1991.28.593 (pl. 40)

ROBERT BECHTLE (b. 1932)
Four Palm Trees, 1969
Oil on canvas, 45 x 52 in. (114.3 x 132.1 cm)
Museum purchase, American Art Trust Fund
2012.43 (pl. 41)

ALBERT BIERSTADT (1830–1902)
California Spring, 1875
Oil on canvas, 54 1/4 x 84 1/4 in. (137.8 x 214 cm)
Presented to the City and County of San Francisco by Gordon Blanding
1941.6 (pl. 1)

BERNICE BING (1936–1998)
Mayacamas No. 6, March 12, 1963, 1963
Oil on canvas, 49 x 48 in. (124.5 x 121.9 cm)
Gift of the Estate of Bernice Bing
1999.148 (pl. 28)

SANDOW BIRK (b. 1962)
Fog over San Quentin State Prison, San Quentin, California, from the series *Prisonation*, 2001
Oil and acrylic on canvas, 66 x 90 in. (167.6 x 228.6 cm)
Museum purchase, American Art Trust Fund
2002.7 (pl. 49)

ELMER BISCHOFF (1916–1991)
Yellow Lampshade, 1969
Oil on canvas, 70 x 80 in. (177.8 x 203.2 cm)
Museum purchase, gift of Nan Tucker McEvoy in memory of her mother, Phyllis de Young Tucker
1992.10 (pl. 33)

MATT BLACK (b. 1970)
Riding to Work in a Farm Labor Bus, Fresno, California, 2004, printed 2016
Ink-jet print on Museo Silver Rag paper, 13 3/8 x 20 in. (34 x 50.8 cm)
Museum purchase, gift of the Docent Council Commemorative Fund to honor the 50th anniversary of the Docent Council
2016.23.3 (pl. 43)

JOAN BROWN (1938–1990)
Young Girl, 1962
Enamel paint on canvas, 48 x 36 in. (121.9 x 91.4 cm)
Gift of Morgan and Betty Flagg in memory of his mother, Mabel R. Flagg
2005.92.1 (pl. 31)

ALFRED RAY BURRELL (1877–1952)
Eucalyptus, Berkeley Hills, 20th century
Drypoint, 9 x 13 in. (22.8 x 32.9 cm)
California State Library long loan
L1966.1319 (pl. 23)

IMOGEN CUNNINGHAM (1883–1976)
Untitled (Ruth Asawa kneeling on floor of dining room with tied wire sculpture), 1963
Gelatin silver print, 9 x 7 3/4 in. (22.9 x 19.7 cm)
Gift of Ruth Asawa and Albert Lanier
2006.114.5 (pl. 38)

JAY DEFEO (1929–1989)
Mountain No. 2, 1955
Oil on canvas, 46 x 36 in. (116.8 x 91.4 cm)
Museum purchase, gift of the Friends of New Art
1995.2 (pl. 27)

RICHARD DIEBENKORN (1922–1993)
Berkeley #3, 1953
Oil on canvas, 58 x 72 1/2 x 3 1/2 in. (147.3 x 184.2 x 8.9 cm)
Bequest of Josephine Morris
2003.25.3 (pl. 29)

RICHARD DIEBENKORN (1922–1993)
Ocean Park #116, 1979
Oil and charcoal on canvas, 81 1/4 x 72 in. (206.5 x 182.9 cm)
Museum purchase, gift of Mrs. Paul L. Wattis
2000.20 (pl. 30)

AMOS WILLIS ENGLE (1880–1926)
Docks at Monterey, early 20th century
Woodcut, 9 x 6 in. (22.9 x 15.3 cm)
Gift of Robert Neuhaus
1965.58.11 (pl. 13)

GEORGE FISKE (1835–1918)
Glacier Point, Yosemite, ca. 1880
Albumen silver print, 7 1/2 x 4 1/4 in. (19.1 x 10.8 cm)
Gift of Dr. and Mrs. Steven Nash
1996.151.1 (pl. 3)

JAMES EDWARD FITZGERALD (1899–1971)
Artichoke Ranch, 1939
Watercolor on paper, 19 5/8 x 24 7/16 in. (49.8 x 62 cm)
Allocated by the Federal Art Project
L43.2.844 (pl. 44)

FRANK MORLEY FLETCHER (1866–1949)
California 1—Salinas River, 1927–1928
Color woodcut on Japanese paper, 12 13/16 x 17 1/16 in. (32.5 x 43.3 cm)
California State Library long loan
L77.1966 (pl. 11)

E. CHARLTON FORTUNE (1885–1969)
Summer Night, 1920
Oil on canvas, 45 x 50 in. (114.3 x 127 cm)
Partial gift of Glenn L. and Jane Fortune Hickerson
2003.165 (pl. 19)

FRANCES HAMMEL GEARHART (1869–1958)
The Boat Pier, 19th–20th centuries
Color woodcut, 9 x 6 5/8 in. (22.9 x 16.7 cm)
California State Library long loan
L401.1966 (pl. 14)

FRANCES HAMMEL GEARHART (1869–1958)
Low Tide, 1930
Color woodcut, 10 1/16 x 11 in. (25.6 x 28 cm)
California State Library long loan
L397.1966 (pl. 15)

SELDEN CONNOR GILE (1877–1947)
Spring, 1928
Oil on canvas, 24 x 30 in. (61 x 76.2 cm)
Museum purchase, gift of Jane Newhall
2001.66 (pl. 5)

TEIKICHI HIKOYAMA (1884–1957)
Mt. Tamalpais, 1927
Oil on canvas, 16 x 20 in. (40.6 x 50.8 cm)
Museum purchase, Volunteer Council Art Acquisition Fund
2016.18 (pl. 7)

CLARK HOBART (1868–1948)
The Blue Bay: Monterey, ca. 1914
Oil on canvas, 20 1/4 x 24 1/4 in. (51.4 x 61.6 cm)
Museum purchase, Skae Fund Legacy
41772 (pl. 17)

DAVID HOCKNEY (b. 1937)
Mulholland Drive, June 1986, 1986
Color xerographic print, 11 x 17 in. (27.9 x 43.2 cm)
Anderson Graphic Arts Collection, gift of the Harry W. and Mary Margaret Anderson Charitable Foundation
1996.74.187 (pl. 48)

WILLIAM KEITH (1839–1911)
Hetch Hetchy Side Canyon, I, ca. 1908
Oil on canvas, 22 x 28 in. (55.9 x 71.1 cm)
Presented to the City and County of San Francisco by Gordon Blanding
1941.4 (pl. 4)

WILLIAM KEITH (1839–1911)
Spring Landscape (Spring in Marin County), 1893
Oil on canvas, 30 x 47 in. (76.2 x 119.4 cm)
Gift of Mrs. Walter Martin in memory of Henry T. Scott
50.6 (pl. 2)

DONG KINGMAN (1911–2000)
Coit Tower and Embarcadero, ca. 1935–1943
Watercolor on paper, 20 x 28 in. (50.8 x 71.1 cm)
Allocated by the Federal Art Project
L43.2.889 (pl. 26)

L.A. FINE ARTS SQUAD (1969–1972)
VICTOR HENDERSON (b. 1939)
TERRY SCHOONHOVEN (1945–2001)
Isle of California: Lunch Brake for V. Henderson and T. Schoonhoven, 1973
Lithograph printed in brown with watercolor additions, 28 1/8 x 35 11/16 in. (71.4 x 90.6 cm)
Museum purchase, Achenbach Foundation for Graphic Arts Endowment Fund
1974.13.26 (pl. 47)

PAUL LANDACRE (1893–1963)
Edge of the Desert, plate XI in the book *California Hills and Other Wood Engravings* (Los Angeles: Bruce McCallister, 1931), 1931
Wood engraving, 12 3/4 x 9 3/4 in. (32.4 x 24.8 cm)
A102925 (pl. 10)

ALMA LAVENSON (1897–1989)
Eucalyptus Leaves, 1933, printed 1987
Gelatin silver print, 14 x 11 in. (35.6 x 27.9 cm)
Gift of Francisco Gaona and Jane Lukens
2008.69.10 (pl. 37)

PEDRO J. LEMOS (1882–1954)
The Path to the Sea, ca. 1915
Color woodcut on Japanese paper, 10 1/8 x 7 1/2 in. (25.7 x 19.1 cm)
Museum purchase, Achenbach Foundation for Graphic Arts Endowment Fund
1987.1.37 (pl. 21)

MICHAEL LIGHT (b. 1963)
Mono Craters 07.17.06 #10: Burned Jeffrey Pine Forest and Tephra Flow Looking Southeast, Highway 120 at Right, Mono Basin, California, 2006
Inkjet print on paper, 40 x 50 in. (101.6 x 127 cm)
Museum purchase, gift of Dagmar and Ray Dolby
2008.3.1 (pl. 45)

HELEN LUNDEBERG (1908–1999)
Waterways III, 1962
Oil on canvas, 50 x 50 in. (127 x 127 cm)
Gift of the Estate of Moses and Ruth Helen Lasky, San Francisco
Harlan B. and Marshall P. Levine, trustees
2005.147.2 (pl. 35)

RICHARD MAYHEW (b. 1924)
Rhapsody, 2002
Oil on canvas, 48 x 60 in. (121.9 x 152.4 cm)
Museum purchase, Volunteer Council Art Acquisition Fund
2010.2 (pl. 6)

RICHARD MISRACH (b. 1949)
Desert Fire #77, 1984
Chromogenic print, 8 7/16 x 10 15/16 in. (21.5 x 27.8 cm)
Gift of Bill Stimson
2004.18 (pl. 46)

GORDON MORTENSEN (b. 1938)
The Big Sur River, 1978
Color woodcut, 22 1/8 x 30 in. (56.2 x 76.1 cm)
Gift of ADI Gallery
1978.1.143 (pl. 24)

CHIURA OBATA (1885–1975)
Lake Basin in the High Sierra, ca. 1930
Ink and color on silk mounted on paper, 69 1⁄2 x 102 1⁄2 in. (176.5 x 260.4 cm)
Museum purchase, Dr. Leland A. and Gladys K. Barber Fund
2000.71.1 (pl. 8)

DAVID PARK (1911–1960)
Two Bathers, 1958
Oil on canvas, 49 1⁄4 x 55 3⁄8 in. (125.1 x 140.7 cm)
Gift of Deborah G. Seymour
2009.73 (pl. 32)

CHARLES ROLLO PETERS (1862–1928)
By Monterey Bay, ca. 1895
Oil on canvas, 21 3⁄8 x 26 5⁄8 in. (54.3 x 67.6 cm)
Gift of Christine Clark
2006.77 (pl. 20)

ROLAND PETERSEN (b. 1926)
Palm Sunday, 1966
Oil and synthetic resin on canvas, 72 x 68 1⁄8 in. (182.9 x 173 cm)
Gift of Roland Petersen
68.13 (pl. 34)

GOTTARDO PIAZZONI (1872–1945)
Untitled (Seacliff and Trees), ca. 1910
Monotype, 5 x 6 1⁄2 in. (12.7 x 16.5 cm)
Gift of the M.H. de Young Museum Society
53.9.52 (pl. 16)

JOSEPH M. RAPHAEL (1869–1950)
San Francisco Beach with Amusement Park, Opposite of Hills in Marin County, 1939–1950
Color woodcut, 12 1⁄8 x 22 3⁄4 in. (30.9 x 57.7 cm)
Achenbach Foundation for Graphic Arts
1963.30.3538 (pl. 25)

WILLIAM SELTZER RICE (1873–1963)
Windblown Cypress Trees, 1930
Color woodcut on Japanese paper, 9 x 12 in. (22.9 x 30.5 cm)
California State Library long loan
L292.1966 (pl. 22)

CHARLES DORMAN ROBINSON (1847–1933)
Cypress Point, Monterey County, 1909
Oil on canvas, 16 1⁄4 x 20 1⁄8 in. (41.3 x 51.1 cm)
Gift of George H. Kahn
47595 (pl. 18)

ED RUSCHA (b. 1937)
A Particular Kind of Heaven (middle panel), 1983/2005
Oil on canvas, each panel 90 × 136 1⁄2 in. (228.6 × 346.7 cm)
Museum purchase, Mrs. Paul L. Wattis Fund, Foundation purchase, Phyllis C. Wattis Fund for Major Accessions
2001.85, 2005.20a–b (pl. 50)

JOHN SACCARO (1913–1981)
Blue Hills, 1940
Watercolor over traces of graphite pencil on paper, 22 13⁄16 x 30 1⁄2 in. (58 x 77.5 cm)
Allocated by the Federal Art Project
L43.2.923 (pl. 9)

WAYNE THIEBAUD (1920–2021)
Ponds and Streams, 2001
Acrylic on canvas, 72 x 60 in. (182.9 x 152.4 cm)
Museum purchase, gift of Richard N. Goldman
2001.168 (pl. 42)

ARTHUR TRESS (b. 1940)
Untitled (Coit Tower), from the series *San Francisco*, 1964, printed 2010–2011
Selenium-toned gelatin silver print, 14 x 11 in. (35.6 x 27.9 cm)
Gift of Steven Rifkin and Nicole Browning
2011.27.51 (pl. 39)

YU-HO TSENG (1924–2017)
Mural #2, from *Western Frontier*, 1964
Twelve-panel mural; palladium and gold leaf, handmade paper, tapa cloth, and acrylic paint mounted on hardboard, 115 x 153 x 1 3⁄4 in. (292.1 x 388.6 x 4.4 cm)
Gift of Wachovia Corporation
2008.76.2.1–12 (pl. 36)

UNIDENTIFIED ARTIST (active twentieth century)
California Dream, ca. 1925–1940
Color offset lithograph, 9 7⁄8 x 10 13⁄16 in. (25.1 x 27.5 cm)
Museum purchase, Achenbach Foundation for Graphic Arts Endowment Fund
1976.1.184 (pl. 12)

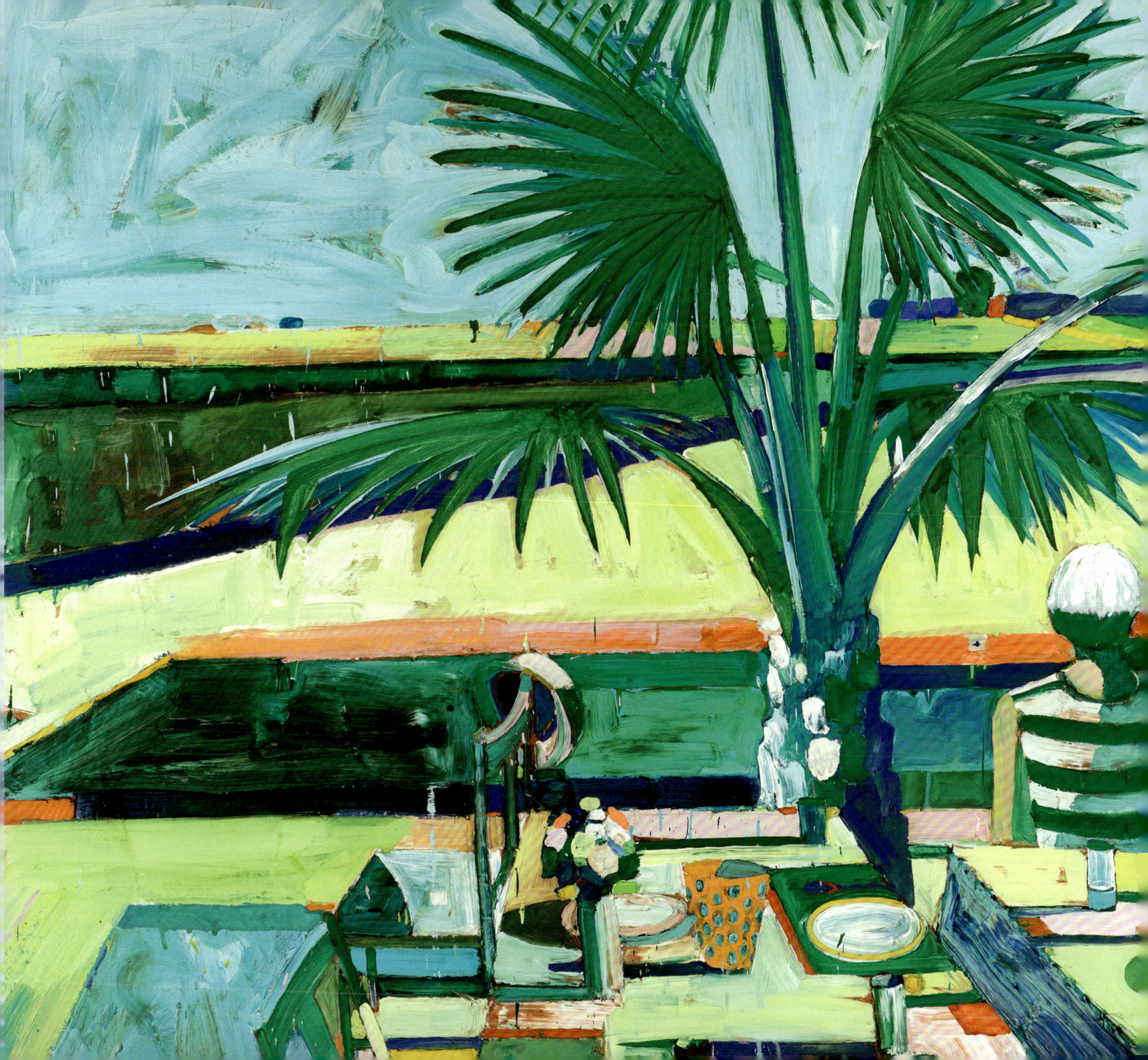

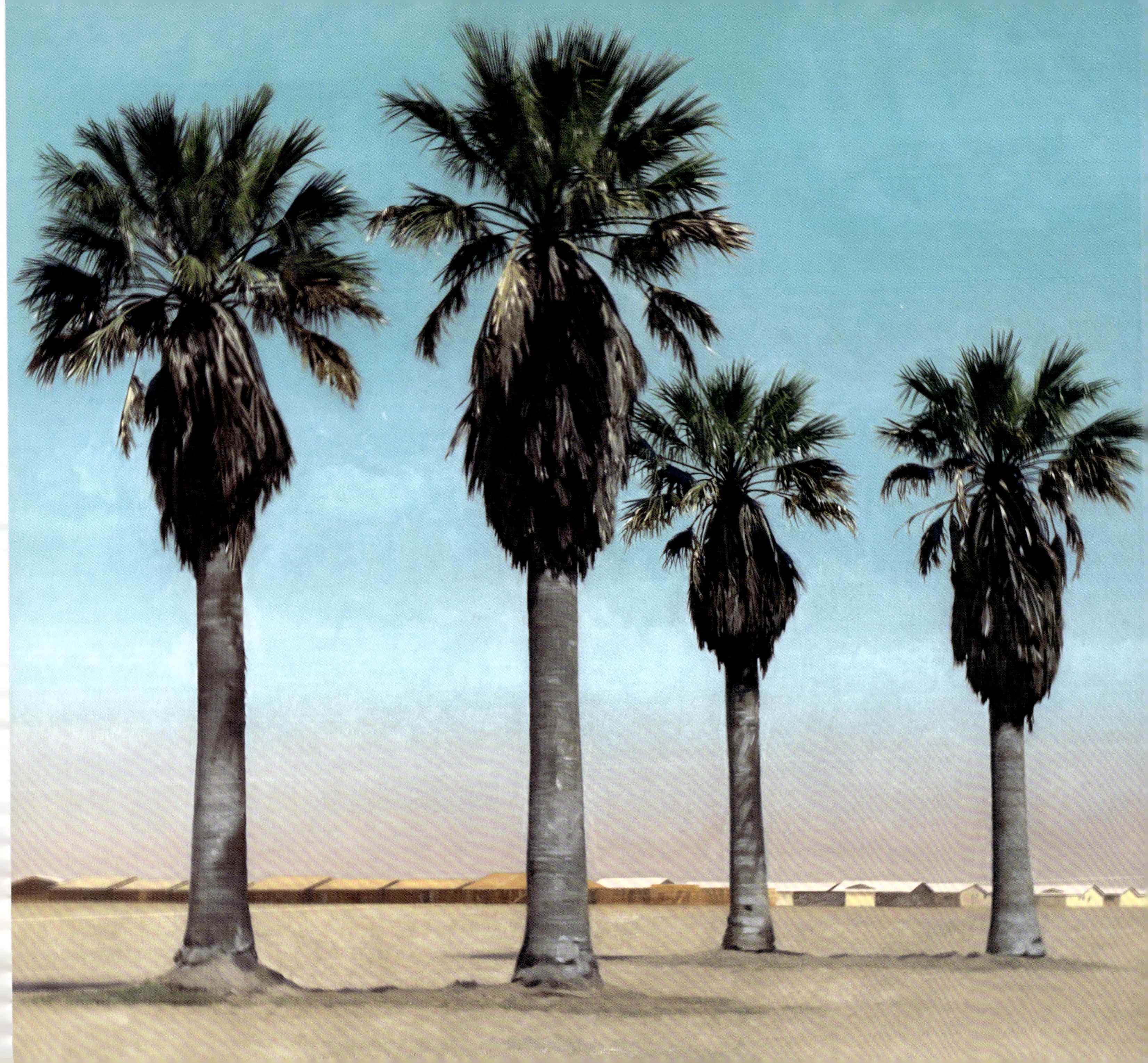

PICTURE CREDITS

ESSAY ILLUSTRATIONS: 1: Federal Art Project, photograph by Jorge Bachmann / Fine Arts Museums of San Francisco (FAMSF); 2, 6: Photograph by Randy Dodson / FAMSF; 3, 5: Photograph by Joseph McDonald / FAMSF, scan by Krause Johansen; 4: Photograph by Joseph McDonald / FAMSF; 7: Copyright © Estate of John Langley Howard, photograph by Randy Dodson / FAMSF; 8: Copyright © Bob Schnepf, photograph by Jorge Bachmann / FAMSF; 9: Copyright © Rupert Garcia, photograph by Randy Dodson / FAMSF; 10: Copyright © Wayne Thiebaud Foundation / Licensed by VAGA at Artists Rights Society (ARS), New York, photograph by Randy Dodson / FAMSF; 11: Copyright © Ed Ruscha, photograph by Joseph McDonald / FAMSF.

GALLERY ILLUSTRATIONS: 1–4, 7, 12–13, 16–17, 19–21: Photograph by Randy Dodson / Fine Arts Museums of San Francisco (FAMSF); 5, 24: Courtesy of the artist, photograph by Randy Dodson / FAMSF; 6: Copyright © Richard Mayhew, photograph by Randy Dodson / FAMSF; 8: Copyright © Estate of Chiura Obata, photograph by Joseph McDonald / FAMSF, scan by Krause Johansen; 9: Copyright © Estate of John Saccaro, photograph by Joseph McDonald / FAMSF; 10: Copyright © 2023 Estate of Paul Landacre / Licensed by VAGA at Artists Rights Society (ARS), New York, photograph by Randy Dodson / FAMSF; 11: Courtesy of the California State Library, photograph by Joseph McDonald / FAMSF; 14–15: Copyright © Estate of Frances Hammel Gearhart, Courtesy of the California State Library, photograph by Randy Dodson / FAMSF; 18: Photograph by Joseph McDonald / FAMSF; 22: Courtesy of the Estate of William Seltzer Rice, photograph by Randy Dodson / FAMSF; 23: Copyright © Estate of Alfred Ray Burrell, photograph by Randy Dodson / FAMSF; 25: Copyright © Estate of Joseph M. Raphael, photograph by Randy Dodson / FAMSF; 26: Copyright © The Don Kingman Estate, photograph by Randy Dodson / FAMSF; 27: Copyright © 2023 The Jay DeFeo Foundation / Artists Rights Society (ARS), New York, photograph by Joseph McDonald / FAMSF, scan by Krause Johansen; 28: Copyright © Estate of Bernice Bing, photograph by Randy Dodson / FAMSF; 29–30: Copyright © Richard Diebenkorn Foundation, photograph by Dick Grant; 31: Copyright © Estate of Joan Brown, photograph by Jorge Bachmann / FAMSF; 32: Copyright © Estate of David Park, photograph by Randy Dodson / FAMSF; 33: Copyright © Estate of Elmer Bischoff, photograph by Joseph McDonald / FAMSF; 34: Copyright © Roland Petersen and Caryl Petersen, photograph by Randy Dodson / FAMSF; 35: Copyright © The Feitelsen / Lundeberg Art Foundation, photograph by Joseph McDonald / FAMSF; 36: Copyright © Estate of Yu-ho Tseng, photograph by Joseph McDonald / FAMSF; 37: Copyright © Estate of Alma Lavenson, photograph by Randy Dodson / FAMSF; 38: Copyright © Imogen Cunningham Trust. Artwork copyright © 2023 Ruth Asawa Lanier, Inc. / Artists Rights Society (ARS), New York, courtesy of David Zwirner, photograph by Randy Dodson / FAMSF; 39: Copyright © Arthur Tress Archive LLC1964, photograph by Robert Hennessey; 40: Copyright © Iain Baxter&, photograph by Jorge Bachmann / FAMSF; 41: Courtesy of the artist and Gallery Paule Anglim, San Francisco, photograph by Randy Dodson / FAMSF; 42: Copyright © Wayne Thiebaud Foundation / Licensed by VAGA at Artists Rights Society (ARS), New York, photograph by Joseph McDonald / FAMSF; 43: Matt Black / Magnum Photos, courtesy of Robert Koch Gallery, photograph by Jorge Bachmann / FAMSF; 44: Copyright © Estate of James Edward Fitzgerald, Monhegan Museum of Art & History, photograph by Randy Dodson / FAMSF; 45: Courtesy of the artist and Michael Light Studio, photograph by Randy Dodson / FAMSF; 46: Copyright © Richard Misrach 2023, photograph by Randy Dodson / FAMSF; 47: Courtesy of the L.A. Fine Arts Squad, photograph by Randy Dodson / FAMSF; 48: Copyright © David Hockney, photograph by Richard Schmidt; 49: Copyright © Sandow Birk, courtesy of the artist and Catharine Clark Gallery, San Francisco, photograph by Joseph McDonald / FAMSF; 50: Copyright © Ed Ruscha, photograph by Randy Dodson / FAMSF

de Young \ \ Legion of Honor fine arts museums of san francisco

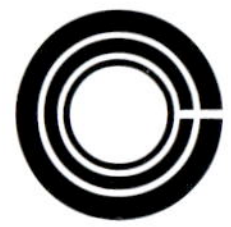

Fine Arts Museums of San Francisco
de Young, Golden Gate Park
50 Hagiwara Tea Garden Drive
San Francisco, CA 94118-4502
www.famsf.org

Leslie Dutcher, director of publications
Trina Enriquez, senior editor
Victoria Gannon, senior editor
Lesley Bruynesteyn, editor
José Jovel, publications associate
Kristi Mitsuda, associate editor

CAMERON + COMPANY
an imprint of ABRAMS
www.cameronbooks.com

Project management and editing by Trina Enriquez
Proofread by Victoria Gannon with Kristi Mitsuda
Picture research by José Jovel with Britta Traub
Designed by Leslie Dutcher and Matt Mayerchak
Color separations by Rusty Sena, Art Product
Printing and binding by Conti Tipocolor, Italy

Library of Congress control number: 2023933493

ISBN: 978-1-949480-41-2

ARTISTIC CALIFORNIA

is published by the Fine Arts Museums of San Francisco and CAMERON + COMPANY to document and celebrate works of California-themed art held in the Museums' permanent collection.